David le Marchand 1674-1726
'An Ingenious Man for Carving in Ivory'

'Mr Marchand an Ingenious Man for carving in Ivory, born at Dieppe has been many years in England, done a vast number of heads from ye life in basso relief some statues in Ivory, his picture painted by Highmore.'

George Vertue (1684-1756), *Notebooks*

Charles Avery

David le Marchand 1674-1726

'An Ingenious Man for Carving in Ivory'

Lund Humphries Publishers London

First published in 1996 by
Lund Humphries Publishers Limited
Park House
1 Russell Gardens
London NW11 9NN

on the occasion of the exhibition
David Le Marchand (1674-1726): 'An Ingenious Man for Carving in Ivory'
National Gallery of Scotland, Edinburgh 7 March-6 May 1996
British Museum, London 23 May-15 September 1996
Leeds City Art Gallery 2 October 1996-5 January 1997

British Library Cataloguing in Publication Data
A catalogue record of this book is available from the British Library

ISBN 0 85331 686 4

Distributed in the USA by
Antique Collectors' Club
Market Street Industrial Park
Wappingers Falls
NY12590
USA

Designed by Alan Bartram
House Editor: Lucy Myers
Copy-editor: Charlotte Burri
Typeset in Monotype Columbus
Made and printed in Great Britain by
BAS Printers Limited
Over Wallop, Stockbridge, Hampshire

HALF-TITLE ILLUSTRATION
*Self-portrait(?) c.*1710 (Cat.61)

Contents

IN MEMORIAM

D.C.A.   **R.F.A.**
(6·I·1902 − 6·X·1993)   (26·I·1911 − 19·IX·1993)

†

D.L.W.   **H.C.W.**
(23·VIII·1910 − 3·VI·1995)   (6·X·1910 − 15·III·1994)

Acknowledgements

The author and publishers would like to thank the following sponsors for their generous financial support, without which this catalogue raisonné could not have come into being:

W. & F. C. Bonham & Sons Ltd
The Idlewild Trust
The Paul Mellon Centre for Studies in British Art
The Henry Moore Foundation
The Scouloudi Foundation in association with the Institute of Historical Research
John Lewis Esq
Christopher Loyd Esq MC DL JP
Sotheby's
Lord Thomson of Fleet

Thanks are also due to the following who kindly advised on the raising of these funds:

Dr Brian Allen
Professor Geoffrey Beard
Timothy Llewellyn Esq
Dr Tessa Murdoch
Randolph Vigne Esq

The author would like to thank all those colleagues, friends and owners of ivory carvings, who are too numerous to mention, but who over the years have liberally contributed information and supplied photographs and documentation that have helped to build up the present picture of David Le Marchand's life and artistic achievement. It is hoped that this catalogue will bring them pleasure and be a sufficient recompense.

The following however deserve to be singled out as prime movers:

Terence Hodgkinson
John Kerslake
Christian Theuerkauff
Lord Thomson of Fleet
Elizabeth Wilson
Reiner Winkler

The author is also grateful to the following museum colleagues who espoused so readily and promoted so vigorously the concept of a monographic exhibition on Le Marchand in 1996:

Neil Stratford and Aileen Dawson, The British Museum
Terry Friedman and Adam White, Leeds City Art Galleries
Robert Hopper and Penelope Curtis, The Henry Moore Institute, Leeds
Timothy Clifford and Helen Smailes, National Gallery of Scotland

Thanks are also due to the publishers, Lund Humphries, whose Director Lionel Leventhal and Managing Editor Lucy Myers determined with enthusiasm to adopt the project and to see it through to such a satisfactory conclusion. I am grateful to Charlotte Burri for her punctilious and enthusiastic copy-editing and to Alan Bartram for an elegant and economical design.

Photographic Credits

David Le Marchand: Chronology

1674   12 October: David Le Marchand born in Dieppe, son of Guillaume, a painter

1683   [Jean Cavalier, ivory carver of French origin, naturalised in London]

1684   [Jean Cavalier dates *King Charles II* (ill.p.16)]

1685   [Revocation of the Edict of Nantes]
[Accession of King James II & VII]

1688   [Flight of King James II into exile; Glorious Revolution; accession of King William III and Queen Mary]
[Jean Cavalier dates *Pepys* (ill.p.74)]

1689   Portrait medallion of (?) Vauban, signed 'Le Marchand' (Cat.1)

1694   [Bombardment of Dieppe by the British and the Dutch. Dieppe is half destroyed]

1696   12 February: Le Marchand permitted to open a shop in Edinburgh (see ill.p.14)
Portrait medallion of James Mackenzie (Cat.8)
[Isaac Newton moves to London as Master of the Mint]

1697?   Bust of John Locke ('Aetat 65') (see Cat.69)

1698   [François Le Pipre, portrait painter and modeller in wax, dies: *terminus ante quem* for the wax model of Thomas Guy (Cat.43)]

1699   [Anne Churchill marries the Earl of Sunderland: Le Marchand's busts of her possibly date from this year (Cats 24-6)]
[Act of Parliament forbidding the use and wear of Eastern silk: provides a *terminus ante quem* for the portrait medallion of a *Gentleman in a Banyan* (Cat.19)]
[Jean Cavalier dies in Isfahan]

1700   David le Marchand probably comes to London, following Jean Cavalier's death
Bust of an *Anonymous Nobleman* ('Grand Dauphin') (Cat.29)
Portrait medallion of Elizabeth Eyre (Cat.73)
Portrait medallion of Charles Chester Eyre (Cat.75)

1701   Bust of Anne Nelthorpe (Cat.77)

1702   Bust of John Vesey, Archbishop of Tuam (Cat.38)
[Isaac Newton sits to Godfrey Kneller (principal painter to the king). Possible occasion for the portrait plaque (Cat.44)]

[Accession of Queen Anne]

1703   [Samuel Pepys dies; Isaac Newton elected President of the Royal Society]

1704   Bust of Francis Sambrooke (Cat.58)
Bust of an *Anonymous Gentleman* (Cat.78)
[John Locke dies]

1705/6   D. or David Le Marchand, stands godfather to Huguenot infants (see ill.p.18)
[Isaac Newton knighted]

1706   Bust of Lord John Somers (Cat.37)

1709   David Le Marchand naturalised in London (see ill.p.18)

1711   Portrait medallion of Louisa, Countess of Berkeley in the style of Le Marchand (Cat.27)
[J. Dubberman (Jacob Dobbermann, 1682-1745), ivory carver, appears in Kneller's academy and as a member of the Rose & Crown Club in London]

1712   Portrait medallion of Gamaliel Voyce (Cat.59)
[Sir John Houblon (see Cat.70) dies]

1714   Bust of Sir Isaac Newton (Cat.47)
[Queen Anne dies and George I accedes: *terminus post quem* for bust and medallions of *King George I* (Cats 31-5)]

1716   [Anne Churchill, Countess of Sunderland dies; Moses Raper (see Cat.65) and Sir Humphry Morice (see Cat.71) elected as Directors of the Bank of England]

1718   Second bust of Sir Isaac Newton (Cat.68)

1719   Portrait medallion of John Flamsteed (Cat.52)

1720   Portrait relief of Matthew Raper III FRS (Cat.64)
[Anne Dacier dies]
[The South Sea Company bubble bursts: Thomas Guy makes £160,000; Newton loses £20,000]

1721   [Thomas Guy founds his hospital]

1722   11 July: Documented sitting of the Reverend William Stukeley to Le Marchand (see Cat.54)
[The Duke of Marlborough dies]

1723   [Sir Christopher Wren dies, aged ninety-one]

1724   [Thomas Guy dies]

1726   3 February: Le Marchand admitted to French Hospital in London
17 March: Le Marchand dies in hospital

1727   [King George I dies; Sir Isaac Newton dies]

David Le Marchand: Dieppe, Edinburgh, London

Joseph Vernet, *View of the Port of Dieppe*, detail, with a pedlar selling ivories in the
left foreground, oil on canvas, 1765. Musée de la Marine, Paris.

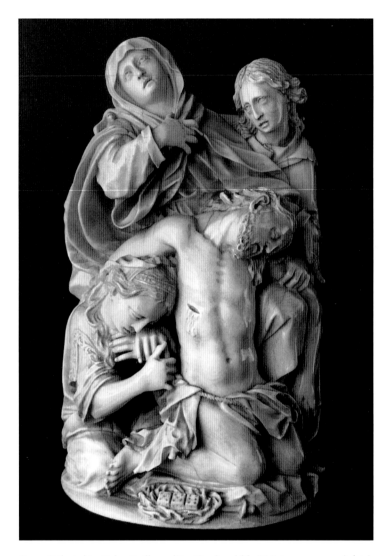

Here attributed to C. (or Guillaume) Le Marchand (?), *Pietà*, ivory 23.5 cm ($9\frac{1}{4}$ in) high. Initialled C. (or G.) L.M. Musée des Arts Décoratifs, Paris (Inv.no. D33465).

Le Marchand's Career

David Le Marchand was born in Dieppe on 12 October 1674. His father Guillaume, an accredited local painter, had married Madeleine Levasseur on 29 July 1658, signing the register in handsome script and appending – curiously enough – a drawing of a human ear (ill.).[1] In Dieppe, several painted altarpieces signed 'G. le marchand' survive, but apart from one depicting *The Circumcision of Christ* in St-Rémy, signed in 1679, it is not clear which are by David's father, and which are by his younger brother (also Guillaume), who lived from 1673 to 1719.[2] Whether David learned to paint we do not know, for his only known works are carved in ivory. They bear witness to the fact that he learned to draw and to observe accurately and perceptively, even if his understanding of figure composition was shaky, perhaps owing to the sheer impossibility of a formal training during his youth (see below). Since the late Middle Ages, Dieppe had become a great centre for ivory carving and turning, and so for an artistic child this craft would have been a natural, alternative avocation.

Indeed, there exists in Paris one work in ivory, a group of the *Pietà* (ill.p.12), that bears the initials 'G(or C).L.M.' rather roughly incised by way of a signature, just as David was to do with his initials 'D.L.M.' later on. In terms of style it appears to date from the middle or end of the seventeenth century, and therefore may have been carved by one of the other Le Marchands, if the first letter is a 'G', by David's father or his brother Guillaume, or if it is a 'C', by another relation: in either case, it may be evidence of a family activity in this field, alongside that of painting. An ivory portrait miniature possibly depicting Vauban and signed 'Le Marchand Fecit. Anno 1689' has also recently come to light in France (Cat.1). It is a tiny *tour de force*, and if the Le Marchand in question is David, he was remarkably precocious, for he would have been only fifteen. The curls of the wig are certainly depicted in a style that was later to be his, so it may be from his hand. Alternatively, if, like the *Pietà*, it was by a close relation, it means that his technique and style were learned at home.

However this may be, David's youth and training remain otherwise completely uncharted, perhaps because of a traumatic event that would have brought turmoil into his parents' life when he was a ten-year-old: the Revocation of the Edict of Nantes in 1685. Freedom of belief was no longer protected, and Huguenot Protestants came once again under official pressure to convert to Roman Catholicism, with dire penalties for non-compliance. The only alternative was to flee secretly to a Protestant country, and many did so, those from Dieppe often making across the Channel to the safe haven of England. Guillaume Le Marchand's reaction to this threat is unknown: if he went into exile in about 1685, he may have taken his wife and children with him, as would be natural. The first that one hears of young David thereafter is in 1696, by which time he was in the United Kingdom: this date follows closely on a second great disaster that befell Dieppe, when in 1694 the Anglo-Dutch fleet bombarded the city and reduced it to ashes, and it may be that he did not leave his native land until then, leaving his brother Guillaume at least to practise painting.

Until recently it was only through documents of the Huguenot community in London from 1705 to 1726, Le Marchand's oath of naturalisation in 1709, and the British subjects of his ivory portraits that

Entry for the marriage of Guillaume Le Marchand and Madeleine Levasseur in the Registers of Dieppe, for 29 July 1658. Archives départementales de la Seine-Maritime, Rouen (5 Mi 1878).

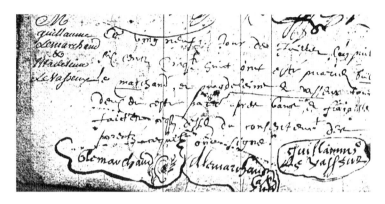

Entry for the baptism of David Le Marchand in the Duplicate Register of the parish church of St-Rémy, Dieppe, for November 1674, giving his date of birth as 12 October. The signature of his father, Guillaume, is followed by a drawing of an ear. Archives municipales de Dieppe, Médiathèque centre Jean Renoir, Dieppe.

his immigration was known. Now, however, in a surprising and fascinating development it has been discovered that in 1696, at the age of twenty-two, he received official permission to practise his craft and open a shop in Edinburgh, on condition that he took on children of local burghers as apprentices (ill.p.14):

'*Licence Lemerchand*
The which day the Council grants Liberty and Licence to David Lemerchand designer and cutter in Ivory to exercise the sd. arte within the good toun & priviledges yr. of & to keep ane open chop for selling of his work belonging to the sd. arte, made by himself or servants allenarly. Upon this express provision that he take & instruct the children of burgeses of this City and other natives of this Kingdome in his sd. arte.

And that he observe the rules & statuts of this City in his imployment, otherwise this presents to be voyd & null. And this act to continue dureing the Councils pleasure.'

It is possible that, having attained his majority, he had emigrated directly to Scotland, along the lines of the Auld Alliance, and not to London via one of the ports opposite Dieppe on the south coast of England – the normal route. There was a small community of Huguenots with a church in Edinburgh where he would have been welcome (see ill.p.15).

How long he benefited from the privileges that he was so generously – and percipiently – accorded in that capital city is not known, but it

Licensing of David Le Marchand, 'designer and cutter in Ivory', to practise his
art and to open a shop in Edinburgh, granted 12 February 1696. Records of the
Burgh of Edinburgh, 1689-1701. Edinburgh City Archives.

seems to have been only for a few years. Eleven ivories with Scottish
subjects have come to light, nine of them so recently as to have remained
unpublished. They place Le Marchand in the forefront of the patronage
that was available there from the nobility, some of whom were, like him,
Protestants, while others were Catholic and Jacobite. A laureate portrait
of that crucial figure, King James II of England and VII of Scotland
(Cat.14), is the most significant addition to David's *oeuvre*,[3] while a
miniature of the titular 2nd Duke of Perth, and a disc bearing his ducal
armorial achievement (Cats 11-13), as well as five portraits of the
Mackenzies at Castle Leod (Cats 6-10), broaden our perception of his
Scottish patronage beyond that of the Earl and Countess of Leven,
whose images have been in the Victoria & Albert Museum since 1956
(Cats 4-5). Heretofore it was assumed that the latter portraits must have
been carved during a visit to London, but their relatively small size and
low degree of relief correspond perfectly with those of the other
Scottish sitters, one of which is dated 1696, the very year in which Le
Marchand opened his shop in Edinburgh. The Scottish portraits (with

the exception of the oval medallion of King James and a miniature bust)
are small and carved from thin plaques of ivory – perhaps all that was
available in Edinburgh, possibly even a stock-in-trade brought from
Dieppe by the sculptor himself. Where signed, it is with minuscule
capital letters.

When did Le Marchand leave Edinburgh for London and its wider
spheres of patronage? He was almost certainly in the metropolis by
1700, for several of his best works depicting English sitters are dated
between then and 1705, when a man of his name first featured in the
Huguenot documentation as witness at a baptism. Indeed, he may have
come down to London as early as 1697, for a lost bust of John Locke
(Cat.69) *may* have been executed then, according to the inscribed age of
the subject. Locke sat to Sir Godfrey Kneller in that very year, and Le
Marchand might have attended the same sittings in order to produce a
wax model (carving a tusk of ivory into a likeness was a laborious
process that would not have been performed in the presence of the
subject, except perhaps for some final touches to enhance it to

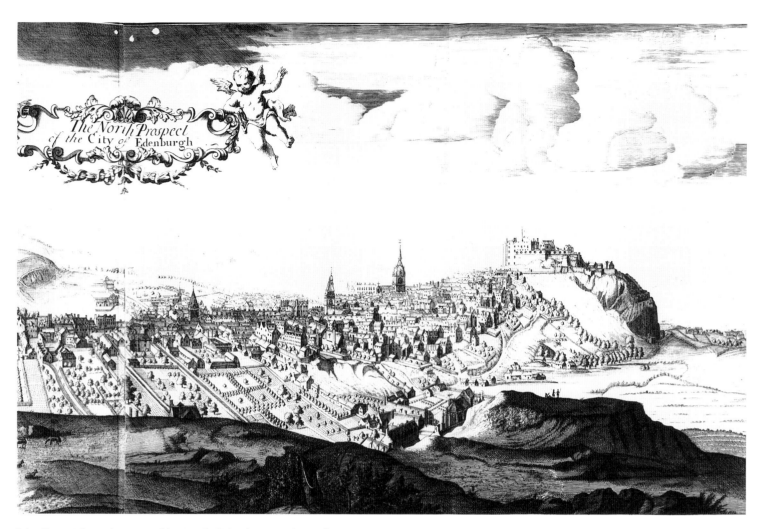

John Slezer, *The North Prospect of the City of Edinburgh*, reprinted 1797 from *Theatrum Scotiae*, c.1700. The Map Library, The National Library of Scotland (EMS b.3.22).

perfection). The portrait seems so incisive as to suggest that it was done from life, and therefore in 1697. While this might seem early in his career to have developed his capacities sufficiently for such a masterly representation, he was to sign and date a brilliant bust of a nobleman in 1700, as well as several others in the next few years.

Nevertheless, one should bear in mind the absence from the inscription of the crucial words '*ad vivum*' – 'from life' – that the carver employed on other occasions, and the fact that it was a normal part of a sculptor's craft to reproduce a sitter's features in three dimensions from an image in only two dimensions – a drawing, painting or engraving. If Le Marchand copied the likeness ('Effigies', as appears in the inscription) of Locke as he appeared in 1697 from Kneller's portrait (or a derivative), he could have done so at any subsequent time, for instance perhaps in 1714 or 1718, the dates on his principal busts of Newton, which are very like it in appearance and size. The inscription would then have no bearing on the date the carver came to London from Edinburgh: indeed, it would be surprising if he had left his new shop there so soon.

The timing of David's journey south may also have been contingent on the death in 1699 of his greatest predecessor as a portraitist in ivory in England, Jean Cavalier. The latter is probably to be identified with a John Cavalier whose name is listed among the denizations of Huguenots in London on 16 May 1683. Nothing is known of Cavalier's age or origins, though it is usually assumed that he came from Dieppe. He could have been born around 1660. His earliest works, a splendid equestrian portrait of King Charles II on a large oval medallion of ivory (ill.p.16) – an image derived from a Great Seal – and a smaller oval of his daughter-in-law, Isabella, Duchess of Grafton, date from the following year, 1684, and place Cavalier securely in the royal circle, as a court portraitist. His very neat, incisive style is close to that of a medallist, and in the ensuing reign of William and Mary, he was appointed as just that, to carve several brilliant medallions of the royal couple (ill.p.16). He also portrayed luminaries, such as his colleague, the Principal Painter, Godfrey Kneller (see Cat.39) and Samuel Pepys (see Cat.40), as well as aristocrats. Cavalier travelled extensively abroad, in Germany and to the

Jean Cavalier, *King William III*, ivory, 9 cm (3½ in) diam. Signed on truncation of shoulder 'C', *c.*1690. Victoria & Albert Museum, London (A.18-1938).

Jean Cavalier, *King Charles II on Horseback*, ivory, 15.2 cm (6 in) high. Signed on the verso 'I. CAVALIER. F. 1684'. Leeds City Art Galleries (Temple Newsam House). Bought with the aid of a Government grant and a contribution from the National Art-Collections Fund (Inv.no. 27/80).

Jean Cavalier, *Queen Mary II*, ivory, 9 cm (3½ in) high. Signed on the verso 'CAVALIER F. 1686'. Victoria & Albert Museum, London (A.201-1929).

courts of Denmark (1691-3) and Sweden (1694/5-1697), and it was on a diplomatic mission from the latter to Russia and Persia that he met his fate in distant Isfahan in May 1699. News of his demise may have filtered through to Edinburgh later that year, opening the way for Le Marchand to go and seek his fortune as Cavalier's successor in London.

Their styles were completely different, for Le Marchand abjured, perhaps deliberately in order to emphasise the contrast, the standard, circular medallic form of portrait in shallow relief, with neatly encircling inscription and projecting rim, that Cavalier had adhered to, preferring a bolder, more sculptural approach. Indeed, his images often stand out to fully half their natural depth in scale – in '*alto-rilievo*', as distinct from '*basso-rilievo*'. He probably made preliminary models from life in wax, and its ductile nature influenced the style of his drapery, which is gouged out in sinuous folds. Flowing locks of hair, especially the fashionable periwigs of his day, were calligraphically rendered, with an almost waxen softness and sheen, serving as a foil for the boldly projecting and incisively chiselled facial features. Furthermore, in defiance of the correct, classicising epigraphy of Cavalier's inscriptions and initials, painstakingly left in relief as he carved the ivory away around them, David incised his, a much simpler method, and with abandon, often

using crude capitals, untoward abbreviations, and an approximation of copper-plate for his lower-case lettering (ill. p.17).[4] David also enjoyed the greater artistic freedom permitted in busts carved fully in the round, from the solid 'meat' of a large elephant's tusk, which would have been very costly on account of its rarity, not to mention the hours of skilled carving required.

Our only indication of the prices that he charged is a posthumous statement that Newton's nephew, Benjamin Smith, 'left a small ivory bust [of his uncle] of admirable workmanship by that celebrated artist, Marchand, which from its elegance, similitude and placid expression is truly valuable. It is said to have cost Sir Isaac one hundred guineas and is specified in an authentic inventory of his effects, taken by virtue of a commission of appraisement in April 1727, now in my possession'.[5] This was probably one of the busts or large reliefs carved in the second decade when he was at the height of his powers. Even so, if the statement is to be believed, this was a truly enormous sum: in the mid-1720s Rysbrack, for example, charged only a third as much (£35) for a life-size bust of Inigo Jones in marble, while his full-length statue of Queen Anne at Blenheim cost the Duchess of Marlborough only £300! It has also been calculated that in the mid-eighteenth century, 'at least £100 was needed to start almost any sort of business'.[6] Perhaps the imported raw material accounted for much of the price, but if Le Marchand's tariff of charges was as high as this, it is strange that he eventually died a pauper in a charity bed at the French Hospital in London.

Once in London, David's talent as a portraitist in the exotic, luxury material rapidly secured his entrée into the patronage of the highest ranks of society under the reigns of Queen Anne and of King George I. He was called upon to portray the monarchs themselves, though at whose behest is not known, and the nobility, for example John Duke of Marlborough and his pretty daughter Anne – toast of the Kit Kat Club – whose marriage in 1691 to Charles Duke of Sunderland may have occasioned no fewer than three miniature portrait busts. Sarah, her glamorous and forceful mother, is missing, unless it is her likeness, very similar to that of Queen Anne, that is recorded in a wax cast in the Wedgwood Museum (Cat.22). The 3rd Earl of Peterborough (Cat.30), possibly the Earl of Oxford, Lord Somers (Cat.37) and an Irish archbishop (Cat.38) were also counted among Le Marchand's sitters.

Le Marchand's 'frenchified' origins endeared him not only to fellow Huguenots in the city of London, but also to Englishmen of the Whig persuasion, including many of the principal intellectuals, artists and businessmen of the day.[7] Some of his several portraits of those 'British Worthies', Locke and Newton, have already been referred to, but he also portrayed the Reverend William Stukeley, latterly friend and doctor of Newton, in classical guise appropriate to an archaeologist (Cat.54), and John Flamsteed, Astronomer Royal, with whom Newton had fallen out (Cat.52). Both Sir Christopher Wren (Cats 48, 67) and his son and biographer (Cat.49) were depicted, the former twice, as well as the diarist Pepys (Cat.40).

Less celebrated parties, sometimes related to one another, with names such as Eyre (Cats 73-5), Nelthorpe (Cat.77) and Sambrooke (Cat.58) also featured on the list of clientèle. The most obviously Huguenot of his subjects was Michael Garnault (Cat.57), member of a veritable dynasty who settled in London and were successful as jewellers and businessmen, while two members of a humbler family called Voyce (Voyez), may have been fellow-craftsmen (Cats 59, 60).

David enjoyed a particularly intimate relationship with the Raper family (Cats 62-3), carving several portraits of them, possibly at the behest of Moses Raper, a rich silkman who in 1716 was elected a Director of the newly founded Bank of England (Cat.65). Moses may also have commissioned two of the busts of Locke and Newton, and a medallion of Wren, as well as an ivory plaque of Thomas Guy, founder of the hospital of which he was a Director (Cat.42). In return, and most unusually, the Rapers numbered a portrait of David, proudly holding his

David Le Marchand, Verso of *Mathew Raper III* (Cat.64), ivory. Inscription, 'Eff[igies] Mathei RAPER juni[or]. Aetat[is] suae 15 An[no]. ad viv[um] scul[psit]' (*ie* 'Likeness of Mathew Raper Junior in the fifteenth year of his age, carved from life'); with his initials D.L.M. and date 1720. Victoria & Albert Museum, London (A.20-1959).

bust of Newton, among those of the family commissioned from Highmore (see front cover and detail: ill. p.21). The youngest of his subjects, Mathew Raper III FRS, whose portrait as a studious teenager now graces the Victoria & Albert Museum, presumably intended to immortalise Le Marchand when in 1765 he presented the family bust of Newton and medallion of Wren to the British Museum (Cat.64).

Le Marchand's statuettes and narrative reliefs are fewer in number than those of the average continental ivory carver, probably because of the British predilection for portraiture, and perhaps because of their expense (if his charge for the bust of Newton is anything to go by). Those that survive are equally balanced between Christian themes typical of his native Dieppe – a group of the *Virgin and Child* (Cat.92), a *Crucified Christ* (Cat.93, with magnificently rendered anatomy) and two or three narrative plaques (one lost) – and mythological subjects – *Venus and Cupid, Apollo with his lyre, Apollo* (Cats 95-7), and a variation on a theme carved on a monumental scale in marble for Versailles by Regnaudin, *Saturn Abducting Cybele* (Cat.3). The last is from a technical point of view a *tour de force*, though one that was not without parallel on the continent. A plaque of *Apollo and the Muses on Mount Parnassus* (Cat.98) has also been attributed rather convincingly to him, as well as a counter-box lid carved with a Jacobite subject (Cat.15).

It is only by inferences drawn from the identities of Le Marchand's clientèle, their positions in society and their known interrelationships that one may gain any impression of his activity: to talk of a career is perhaps a misnomer in the absence of any more substantial data.

The first reference to his presence in London is thought to be an entry in the parish register of the churches of The Tabernacle, Glasshouse Street and Leicester Fields, where, on 27 May 1705, a 'David Lemarchant' acted as godfather to a one-month-old daughter of Alexandre Sigournay, cobbler, of Newport Alley (ill.p.18).[8] Even so, it was not the practice to mention the godfather's occupation, and so one cannot be sure that this David was our '*ivoirier*', although in the absence of other independently recorded candidates of the same christian name it seems reasonably likely. The same is true of the David Le Marchand who signed the Oath Roll of Naturalizations, King's Bench List, in October 1709 (ill.p.18). Here, however, one may draw some comfort

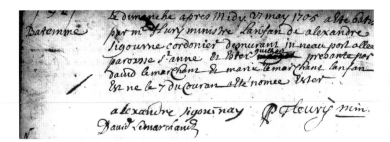

David Le Marchand, signature as godfather at the baptism on 27 May 1705 of Esther, daughter of Alexandre, a cobbler of Newport Alley. Registers of the churches of the Tabernacle Glasshouse Street and Leicester Fields, 1688-1783, folio 92. Public Record Office, London (RG 4/4582).

David Le Marchand, signature on the Oath Roll of Naturalizations, King's Bench List. Dorso of Skin 6 (8 Anno, old No.2). Public Record Office, London (KB 24/2).

D. Marchand (perhaps David Le Marchand), signature as witness of the marriage of Antoine Planck, jeweller, of the Parish of St Leonard Foster and of Madeleine Dubarry of St Paul's, Covent Garden. Register of the church of Swallow Street. Public Record Office, London (RG 4/4609).

from the fact that he signed beneath Mathieu Gosset (1684-1744), who was to make a name for himself in a craft related to that of Le Marchand, modelling life-size waxworks (eg of the French royal family in 1730, wearing their actual clothes of the previous year!), as well as mythological reliefs and portraits in wax, among them King George II and Queen Caroline.[9]

The relative commonness in French of the surname Le Marchand (sometimes spelt with a final 't') makes it dangerous to presuppose that all the Huguenots mentioned in the records of the churches that they frequented were related by family ties. Furthermore, the presence among them of one named Daniel makes for confusion between him and David, when only an initial 'D.' is given in the documents. This is true of what might be a reference to David's presence in London, when a 'D. Marchand' was a witness at the marriage of one Antoine Plank, jeweller, on 3 March 1705/6 in the church in Swallow Street (ill.).

David's name appeared at the baptism of May 1705 alongside that of a godmother who was called Marie Lemarchant, and it is a fair assumption that they were relatives. This is clarified by a reference to a similar occasion in the same church, but nearly ten years later, when on 7 November 1714, a week-old boy was baptised François, for he was son of Mr Daniel and Marie Lemarchant. Marie may therefore have been David's sister-in-law. She was godmother again in May 1719 to baby Elie, son of a Mr Jaques and Mrs Elizabeth Le Marchand, while the godfather was also called Elie, and so the family circle may have been quite extensive. Yet others of the same surname are also recorded.

The most poignant of the Huguenot records are two successive entries in the *Journal des Commissaires* of the French Hospital 'La Providence' for the year 1726, when there were recorded, 'David Marchand Entré le 3 fév.r . . . Sur le Compte de la Corporation', ie at the expense of the charity; and six weeks later, 'David le Marchant mort le 17 Mars . . .'. That this pauper was indeed our ivory carver is confirmed by a friend and medical man whom he had portrayed four years earlier, the Reverend William Stukeley, for he noted in June 1726 the death of 'the famous cutter in ivory Monsr. Marchand, who cut my profile', as well as by the year of death given by Le Marchand's earliest biographer, George Vertue. Thus, while the sculptor's birth in Dieppe and death in London fifty-two years later are exactly attested by documents, almost nothing is known of his life in between, apart from what may be deduced from a consideration of his marvellous surviving works.

Le Marchand, the Raper Family and the Early Bank of England

It sometimes happens that an artist is fortunate enough to find patronage among several members of a particular family, who virtually 'adopt' him out of a due regard for his talents and personality, and that they are instrumental in introducing him to wider patronage among the circles of their friends and business associates. This seems to have been the case with David Le Marchand and a family called Raper, which dwelt near Bishop's Stortford in Hertfordshire and worked in the City of London, prototypes for the modern business commuter, albeit at a slower pace.

The fortunate connection between the sculptor and these patrons was first explored in 1965 by Terence Hodgkinson, when he published the wonderfully vivacious portrait plaque of Mathew Raper III which had been acquired by the Victoria & Albert Museum in 1959 (Cat.64), and by John Kerslake, who followed the ramifications of various Raper family portraits attributable to Highmore and was able to correct a traditional mis-identification (within the family) of one, non-family, figure from Sir Christopher Wren into David Le Marchand (ill.p.21).[1]

Kerslake's convincing identification of the subject has been verified 'officially' by the fact that this portrait has recently been acquired from descendants of the Rapers by the National Portrait Gallery and has been lent in the long term to the British Museum for display near Le Marchand's bust of Newton, which he is seen holding in Highmore's picture, just as many a sculptor used to be depicted holding a hallowed antiquity or a prime example of his own work (see front cover and detail: ill.p.21). There is no need to rehearse Kerslake's subtle lines of argument here: suffice it to say that he worked back conscientiously through the ancestors of the present owners of the real family portraits to the Rapers themselves, and tentatively established their family tree, for the three relevant generations around the year 1700, as discussed below.[2]

From the information given on the reverse of the ivory portrait of the boy, which is inscribed as representing in 1720 Mathew Raper Junior, from life, and aged fifteen, Kerslake established that he was of the third generation in his family in which the eldest son was called Mathew (Cat.64). The earliest, his grandfather, had been born in 1653, son of Thomas Raper (d.1693), Citizen and Grocer of London. Mathew I lived in White Lion Court, Cornhill, and worked as a silk merchant in the parish of St Martin, Ironmonger Lane. He was thus a denizen of the City of London, in which his son and grandsons were to follow him, though they eventually aspired to the gentrification of country houses in Buckinghamshire and Hertfordshire. Mathew I married Elizabeth, c.1674-5, by whom he had two sons, Mathew II and Moses. All three men were elected in due turn Directors of the Bank of England, Mathew I in 1712 until his death a year later; Moses for many three-year periods from 1716 onwards; and Mathew II not until 1730, but thereafter until the year of his death, 1748.

Both brothers were silkmen, and both married daughters of William Billers, Haberdasher of London, Mathew II espousing in 1705 Mary Elizabeth (d.1760), and Moses in 1707 her sister Martha (d.1725). It was Moses, the younger brother, who in 1714 purchased Thorley Court, Hertfordshire, from his father-in-law William Billers, eventually

bequeathing it in 1745 to his brother. Mathew meanwhile lived at Wendover Dean in Buckinghamshire. Moses seems to have had no children and, perhaps having more time on his hands than his elder brother with his seven offspring, and especially after his wife's demise, devoted himself to good works, becoming Governor of St Thomas's and then of Guy's Hospital. He became President of Guy's, served as an executor of Mr Guy's will, and presented an operating theatre in 1739.

This connection makes Moses a possible candidate for the commission to Le Marchand for the ivory relief of Mr Guy (Cat.42), as well as – possibly, in view of its subject – the relief of *The Miracle of Christ healing the Man with the Withered Hand* (Cat.66). Similar scenes of healing cast in bronze feature on the sides of the pedestal of Scheemakers' later monument to the founder in the forecourt of Guy's Hospital (c.1734).[3]

Kerslake very plausibly reorganised the nomenclature traditional within the owners' family of the two principal portraits that are similar in size – and in the probability of Highmore's authorship – to the canvas showing their protégé Le Marchand. The older and more soberly dressed of the two, albeit in a smart coat of velvet, and with his left hand resting nonchalantly on some piece of allegorical relief sculpture of putti, a normal means of indicating cultural aspirations, Kerslake renamed Mathew II. The other, showing a young man with a more truculent and self-satisfied gaze, in a more swaggering pose and with his fine coat drawn apart deliberately to display a luxurious waistcoat of patterned silk, he identified as Moses, possibly painted around the time of his election as Director of the Bank in 1716 (*ie* when he was about thirty-five).

Mathew II would be the obvious candidate to have commissioned the full-length plaque showing his son, Mathew III; however, the recent discovery of a silver medal of King Charles II at the time of the Restoration that is engraved on its rim: 'Matthew Raper born November the 19th 1705. Given him by his uncle Moses Raper Junior 19th November 1706' (ill.p.22), *ie* on the infant's first birthday, indicates a particular avuncular affection.[4] When Moses later found himself childless, this affection for his eldest nephew might have found expression in commissioning the portrait of Mathew II as a diligent student, who also aspired in this 'third' generation to the status of a gentleman scholar of independent means, as distinct from a successful tradesman like his immediate forebears – no Directorship of the Bank of England for him, but rather a fellowship of the Royal Society and assisting at the foundation of a museum!

In any case the Raper brothers of the middle generation both seem to have had portraits made in ivory by Le Marchand, for they are recorded (frustratingly, only at second hand, for the originals are lost) in plaster moulds in the Wedgwood Museum at Barlaston. A pair inscribed on their outsides 'Mr and Mrs Raper' are believed to represent Mathew II and his wife Mary Elizabeth, *née* Billers (1683-1706; *m.*1705) (Cats 62, 63); while another, single item, which is clearly inscribed 'Raper' (twice), also has a less distinct name scratched on it, written smaller, that *might* read 'Moses': the image is similar to that of Mathew, but shows a younger man, and thus is consistent with Highmore's portrait of Moses (see Cat.65). There is no mould at Wedgwood's of Mathew III, but it may have been he who permitted moulds to be taken from the Le Marchand series of family portraits, by then qualifying as 'ancestors', with an ancient Roman sense of filial piety. No original medallions in

Attributed to Joseph Highmore, *Mathew Raper II* (?), *c*.1723, oil on canvas, 127 × 102.6 cm (50 × 40⅜ in). Private Collection.

Attributed to Joseph Highmore, *Moses Raper* (?), *c*.1715, oil on canvas, 125.7 × 101.6 cm (49½ × 40 in). Private Collection.

ceramic by Wedgwood survive, and perhaps none were made, in view of the relative obscurity of their subjects, though modern casts have been produced for purposes of study.

Nevertheless one 'old' cast of Mathew II does exist: faintly initialled 'D.L.M.' below the truncation, it is made of white vitreous paste, probably by the Scot James Tassie, whose favourite material this was for casting reproductions for collectors of ancient and Renaissance gems and cameos etc (Cat.62a). Tassie was closely associated with Wedgwood, and the large medallion of Mathew appeared in the same lot at Christie's as two other smaller ones of later date, depicting William and Elizabeth Raper which are connected undubitably with Tassie, for they appear in catalogues of his *oeuvre*. It is to be hoped that the originals for the moulds by Wedgwood may turn up eventually, perhaps still in the possession of collateral descendants of the Rapers. It may also emerge, given further research, that one or two of the subjects that are now anonymous may have belonged to the same prominent family of patrons (see below pp.100-3).

The historical consciousness of Mathew Raper III also found expression in presenting to the nascent British Museum as early as 1765 two portraits of 'British Worthies' which his family had probably

commissioned. One was a smallish medallion of Sir Christopher Wren, inscribed with his name on its back, which may have given rise to the incorrect, later identification among the family of the figure in Highmore's portrait as Wren also, and not Le Marchand (Cat.67). The other was the magnificent bust of Sir Isaac Newton, dated 1718, which the artist holds in the painting that was so touchingly included among those of the Rapers, as being 'one of the family' (Cat.68).

Mathew was conscious not only of the importance of the two subjects to the culture of their native land, but of the sheer excellence of Le Marchand's depiction, especially in the case of Newton, for it is certainly one of his masterpieces, and one by which he would have wished to be remembered. The Rapers also owned another of the carver's busts, a veritable *tour de force*, and a virtual pair to the Newton, showing John Locke, for their surname is written in ink on its support (Cat.69). Possibly it did not belong to Mathew III, but to one of his relations, for otherwise one might expect him to have given it along with the Newton to the British Museum, where together they would have made a splendid pair.

Of such stuff were the merchant-venturers of the City of London around 1700, living as they did through times of religious and political

Joseph Highmore (1692-1780), *David Le Marchand*, detail, *c.*1723, oil on canvas,
125.7 × 101.6 cm (49½ × 40 in). National Portrait Gallery, London.

turmoil, of burgeoning international trade on a global scale, and of successful business ventures – including the foundation of great institutions, such as the Bank of England, that were fundamental to the emergence of the City of London and thus of the world of modern international business, and of charitable ones, such as Guy's Hospital. The latter has served the poorest denizens of the metropolis well for nearly three centuries until the present day, when it is to be feared that an arrogant disregard for tradition and long service may wantonly bring it down in the name of rationalisation and (falsely directed) economy.

Central to the prosperity of the Rapers was their remunerative business as silkmen. As Earle writes:[5] 'Few importing merchants dealt directly with the final users or consumers of their wares, preferring to sell in bulk to a wholesaler and so turn over their trading capital more rapidly. There were, as a result, specialist wholesalers in every major import trade. One group were the silkmen, who combined dealing in imported raw silk with silk-throwing, selling the final yarn to weavers in London and the provinces.' The end product was of course used in gentlemen's as well as ladies' attire, and as has been remarked, Moses

was self-consciously displaying his own wares and the source of his wealth in revealing the splendour of his waistcoat when he sat – or rather stood – for Highmore.

However, the exponential growth in the fortunes of this astute mercantile clan (which was far from being unique in the competitive City of London of their day) probably stemmed from their participation over two generations in the novel but very profitable venture that was the Bank of England. Today it seems a vast and 'faceless' quasi-national institution, but of course it remains independent of government and its Governor and Court of Directors still wield great power over the economy. But in 1694 the idea of such a bank, founded as a joint venture company, where one could deposit one's spare funds to earn interest from the Government on a continuous basis (funding the National Debt) was distinctly novel, for heretofore this function has been the preserve of the goldsmiths, who had the necessary strong-rooms for the conduct of their own trade, involving as it did precious metals and stones. Indeed they were jealous of their privileges and fought against the foundation of the independent bank.

G. Bowyer, *Restoration of King Charles II*, silver medal, 1660. Edge inscription of 1706 with a dedication from Moses Raper to Mathew Raper III on his first birthday. Victoria & Albert Museum, London (A.6-1992).

The idea was that of a canny Scot, William Paterson, and so one wonders whether virtually from the outset a knowledge of Le Marchand's portraiture in Edinburgh may have been shared by the Court of Directors of the Bank, though no such portrait of Paterson has yet been identified. The Court was to be composed of twenty-four Directors, a Governor and his Deputy, to be elected annually. In order to avoid monopoly and stagnation, it was sensibly decreed that no more than two thirds of the annually retiring Directors might be re-elected, and this accounts for the more or less triennial spells as Director of persons who in fact had a continuing interest in the Bank's affairs such as Moses and Mathew II Raper.[6]

Paterson's scheme for establishing the Bank was preferred to alternative ones by Charles Montagu, a Lord of the Treasury and, from 1694, the year of the foundation of the Bank, Chancellor of the Exchequer. The members of the Court were Protestants to a man, several of them Huguenots, and supporters of the Glorious Revolution of 1688. The Bank was therefore 'a stronghold of the Whigs and a bulwark of the Protestant Succession'.[7]

Amusingly, as it may seem to us today, in view of the Bank's enormous buildings with windowless external walls for the sake of security, it was originally set up in a room in the Mercers' Hall, then moving (1695-1734) to – presumably more spacious – quarters in the Grocers' Hall, as shown in an engraving (ill.), whence eventually it was removed to the grand house in Threadneedle Street of its first Governor, Sir John Houblon (after his widow's demise in 1732), where it has remained, albeit enormously expanded, to the present day.

The closeness of the circle of Directors and their common interest in the commercial success of *their* Bank suggests that they would have got to know each other fairly well and might also have shared the cultural activities expected of well-to-do people, such as commissioning silver plate to enhance their tables and portraits of themselves and their near and dear. As Le Marchand has been proven to be virtually a house-sculptor of portraits to one such family, the Rapers, it seems likely that he might also have served some of their colleagues, perhaps even in the provision of personal mementoes that might be mutually exchanged to the benefit of human relationships.[8]

Anonymous, *Interior of the Bank of England within the Grocers' Hall*, engraving, *c.*1700. The Nuremberg iron strong-box is still in the Bank. Museum and Historical Research Section, Bank of England, London.

Rutger van Langerveldt, German merchants bartering with Africans ingots of
iron for rings of gold and ivory tusks, near Fort Grossfriedrichsburg, Ivory Coast,
drawing in pen, pencil and wash, c.1690. Kupferstichkabinett, Staatliche Museen
Preussischer Kulturbesitz, Berlin (Inv.no. KdZ 13128).

It has emerged that among the anonymous ivory images by Le
Marchand, two are respectably close in appearance to portraits of a
Director of the same generation as Moses Raper, Sir Humphry Morice
(Cat.71), and of the first Governor of the Bank in 1694, who died in
1712, Sir John Houblon (Cat.70).[9] This is not inscribed 'ad vivum' and so
may be a posthumous tribute. These two identifications are presented
here as working hypotheses, untested by time or the criticism of others,
for they were made only during the last stages of the preparation of this
catalogue to coincide with the exhibition in 1996, when the list of
anonymous subjects was focused on, and the ramifications of the
Huguenot connections and Raper presence among the Court of the
Bank of England were comprehensively investigated.

Interestingly enough, the very source of supply of the carver's raw
material may have been via one of these City gentlemen, judging from a

letter written to Sir Humphry Morice, on 17 April 1716[10] (the very year when he was elected to the Court of the Bank of England) from Peter Roberts, one of his agents, at Dickey's Cove on the Guinea Coast about the purchase of '140 Slaves, the most part being men, and I have had ye opportunity of gitting them 4 or 5 pount cheaper than any ship on ye Coast, ye prise when I came from Anomobo was their from 26 to 28 pound for a man slave'. Roberts continued, 'I hearing there is so many Dutch interlopers to windward thatt I shall make ye best of my way to windward to purchase whatt slaves, teeth or malbygete, or what I can geet . . .'.

These teeth were those of the elephant, *ie* tusks of ivory. There is no further reference in any of the letters to Morice from his various ship-captains, but it is likely that such tusks would have stayed on board during the voyage with the slaves to Jamaica and on the return journey, laden with sugar, to Bristol or London, where an owner such as Morice would have had first choice, before selling the remainder of his cargo.

Morice was elected to the Court of the Bank in the same year as Moses Raper, and they may also have been friends and business associates before then. So this is probably the source from which Le Marchand obtained his raw material, at least at the middle stage of his career, when he was carving portraits of several of the City businessmen connected with the Bank of England, including the Rapers, as well as their busts of Newton and Locke (Cats 68, 69). Indeed, the very availability of large tusks direct from Africa, perhaps at a favourable price compared with the market rate, may have encouraged these affluent but canny businessmen to choose ivory, a conspicuously precious commodity, for their portraits, which probably cost far more than those produced with paint on canvas by Highmore and Kneller.

One of the commodities that was being bartered in Guinea against slaves with the native rulers was iron bars: 'He told me he sold 1000 iron barrs at one and a half acky at Whydah. Iron here is much in demand', wrote John Sibson on 12 February 1731;[11] while on 8 June the same year Jonathan Smallwood wrote from Rotterdam, where the ships called on their way from England, 'I have bought ye 400 barrs of Iron at 7f and 1/4 per O, which pleasis Capt. Moore very much'.[12] This suggests that the ingots of triangular cross section that German merchants, who were among the several European rivals of the English over the 'Africa trade', are shown proffering to some Africans in a contemporary watercolour are just such 'iron bars' (ill.p.24). Further research into the details of the ivory market in London is desirable, before jumping to the conclusion that Le Marchand was supplied with raw material only (or principally) via Morice's expeditions and dealings, but it is an attractive working hypothesis nonetheless.

The Art of Ivory Carving

Ivory is the organic material of an elephant's tusk: it is formed out of layer upon layer of dentine, built up round a conoidal nerve cavity, for the tusk is simply an outgrowing canine tooth enlarged by the processes of evolution to serve as an offensive weapon and as a tool. The fine, even grain of this dense material lends itself to carving with sharp tools, drills and abrasives into great detail, while its compact surface may be polished to an appealingly smooth, glossy finish, with a creamy colour uncannily resembling pale human skin.

Ivory has been prized for these qualities and its rarity since the days of the ancient Egyptians: in their paintings and reliefs showing tribute brought down the river Nile from central Africa piles of tusks normally feature alongside ingots of gold. It could also be obtained from the other habitat of the elephant, India. It was always rare and expensive in Europe, so distant from either of these sources of supply, whether by land or sea.

The natural shape of a tusk is awkward for the carver, except when using it to create a huge musical horn (a so-called 'oliphant'), for there are no straight lines or flat surfaces. The tip is solid, but of a curving conical shape, which dictates the forms that can be carved. As the nerve cavity begins to open out inside, but while the walls are still quite thick, flat plaques may be cut along the grain, and these can be cross cut into convenient rectangular shapes, with the off-cuts used for oddly shaped ornaments, inlay or beads.

Finally, the broader lower zone of the tusk becomes ever more hollow and thin-walled, as the diameter of the nerve cavity increases where it approaches the elephant's jaw. Vessels of nearly circular or oval cross section may be cut from that part, as in Byzantine pyxes or the ivory sleeves with friezes of Rubensian figures that were carved in Flanders and Germany during the seventeenth century to fit round great tankards ('*Humpen*'). Otherwise this part may be cut into rectangular but distinctly convex plaques, such as were used for *paxes* or to decorate curved components of saddles, weapons and powder-flasks.

There was a continuous tradition of carving in ivory from the days of ancient Egypt and Greece (Phidias's monumental statue of *Athena* in the Parthenon at Athens was clad in ivory and gold). In the days of the later Roman empire flat plaques were hinged together to form diptychs, with carved designs outside and shallow trays within to contain wax on which to write messages. Once read, these could easily be erased and a reply inscribed with a stylus for return to the sender.

During the Middle Ages, this idea continued, though with Christian scenes: however, alternatively, the outsides were often left plain and the sacred designs were carved instead on the insides for protection, so that when opened they would stand up and function as portable altars (especially useful when on a pilgrimage, crusade or other journey). Images of the *Virgin and Child* could be carved out of the solid, but conoidal and curving, tip of a tusk, and this may have influenced the swaying pose typical of such Gothic figures. Crucifixes could be fashioned by dowelling into the shoulders of the dead Christ arms carved out of separate slivers of ivory (see Cat.93). Secular items such as mirror backs or jewel caskets were often enlivened with chivalrous scenes of sports and pastimes.

After a period of comparative neglect during the Renaissance (possibly owing to a dearth of raw material, caused by the disruption of frequent wars), ivory again became popular in the seventeenth century. While religious imagery always remained a staple product (except in strongly Protestant countries or periods), secular subjects inspired by the Renaissance revival of interest in classical mythology and by popular pastimes such as hunting, courting, feasting and drinking, also became generally acceptable.

The sensuously tactile appearance of polished ivory was exploited by carvers in the Rubensian tradition of Duquesnoy, Petel, Quellinus and Faydherbe, especially for the vivid portrayal of the beauty of nude figures. Moreover, it could also be carved so thinly in relief that the backgrounds became amazingly translucent to set off the drapery, figures and other minute details, as in the virtuoso narrative panels of Van Opstal, Ignaz Elhafen and many other German experts. It continued in popularity for most of the eighteenth century, though, perhaps owing to its high cost, it was gradually supplanted by wax as a medium for portraiture.

With increasing supplies derived from colonial expansion, ivory came into its own once more in the nineteenth century. Initially, like unblemished Carrara white marble, it suited the Neo-classical taste for monochrome purity of surface and idealised contour in statuettes of nude figures, while in England it recommended itself for miniature portrait busts – among them the young Queen Victoria and her Consort Prince Albert – reduced with the help of Cheverton's machine process from life-size busts by sculptors such as Chantrey and Noble. Next, with the Romantic Revival, ivory became a vehicle for all sorts of plaques and figurines in various historical styles from the Gothic to the Baroque, ingeniously carved perhaps, but of precious little aesthetic consequence: Dieppe was responsible for the perpetration of many such monstrosities in poor taste.

Finally, the use of ivory for genuinely original sculpture returned with the Art Nouveau and Art Deco movements, owing to its power to evoke strongly sensuous responses. Bigger tusks imported from the depths of the new colonies in Africa also permitted more ambitious compositions and a more lavish use of the exotic material in most European countries. Occasionally it was combined once again with precious metals, to luxurious effect, in imitation of the 'chryselephantine' technique employed in the ancient world. As late as the 1930s Chiparus was using this technique to advantage, before eventually ivory began to be replaced by the cheaper and more 'modern' cream-coloured plastic, which could readily be moulded and hence mass-produced economically, rather than having to be laboriously and individually carved by hand. Now that the elephant is protected internationally as an endangered species and the raw material available is reduced to only the stock that is already in each country, its use as a material for artistic carving will undoubtedly dwindle away.

Jean-Baptiste Basset, *Grand-Duke Cosimo III of Tuscany*, 1696, ivory, 11.5 cm (4½ in) high. Inscribed on verso, 'JEAN.BAP(TIS)TE BASSET de St Claude en franche comté a fait ce portrait à Livorne ce 2 de mars 1696'. Eugen von Philippovich Collection, Vienna.

A concern for portraying the individual for posterity had been introduced in the Italian Renaissance, with the revival of specifically ancient forms of sculpture such as the marble bust and medallic image in gold, silver or bronze. By the seventeenth century the verisimilitude that could be achieved by carving human features out of ivory ultimately made its use for portraiture inevitable. The smooth polish on the skin of the cheeks, forehead, neck and bosom could be set off to perfection by sharp incisions conveying the hair and costume.

Such portraits were easily portable and when in the form of medallions could be worn like painted miniatures (openly or covertly), or dispatched as tokens of love, loyalty or esteem. They could be mounted for display, for example flanking a fireplace, or concealed in the drawers of a cabinet of curiosities. Small busts could be set on the desk, mantelpiece or dado, or in oval recesses or niches, or between a broken pediment on cabinets, bookcases and similar elegant furniture.

Indeed, portraiture rapidly rose to being one of the highest achievements of sculptors, not only from Dieppe, like David Le Marchand, but all over Europe, and particularly in Germany. Their small scale betokens a particular intimacy, quite different from the more formal demands of life-size portraiture for public contemplation. They have usually been cherished by their owners and occasionally commented upon by discerning friends or visitors.

In the field of portrait medallions, David followed in a local tradition begun at Dieppe in the previous generation by Jean Cavalier and Jean Mancel. By degrees, however, isolated as he was to be in Great Britain, he evolved a highly personal, indeed an indiosyncratic and easily recognisable style, that became ever less medallic, precise and dry and ever more plastic, sculptural and sensuous in feeling.

Le Marchand was no pioneer in the production of portrait busts in ivory in his native France, for at least two good examples by little known, but excellent, French emigré contemporaries exist: one of around 1680 showing a gentleman in a full-bottomed wig, very much in the style of full-scale portraiture in marble at the Court of the Sun King, was signed by a certain C. Lacroix, who had apparently settled in Genoa; while another, surprisingly showing the Grand-Duke Cosimo III of Tuscany, was signed and dated on the back, 'JEAN BAP.TE BASSET de St Claude en franche comté a fait ce portrait à Livorne ce 2 de mars 1696' (ill.p.26).[1] This is written in the same, casual, and deliberately unclassical, approximation of a copper-plate manuscript of the period as David used in several of his longer inscriptions, *eg* on the reverse of the plaque showing Mathew Raper III (Cat.64). These busts are respectively 14.3 cm ($5\frac{1}{2}$ in) and 11.5 cm ($4\frac{1}{2}$ in) high and are thus only slightly smaller than those that Le Marchand was to produce, which are usually 20 cm ($7\frac{7}{8}$ in) high, or more. The additional height of his busts does, however, undoubtedly contribute to their effect, for they are nearly half the size of life. With at least ten such autograph busts to his credit, Le Marchand is by far the most prolific and impressive producer of his day. The majority of busts by his successors as portraitists in England and Germany, the Lücke dynasty, were smaller again, and are perceived as miniatures.

David's busts on the other hand – and some of his larger full-face portraits in high relief – were physically large enough to have impressed several of his successors in the art of life-size portraiture in marble sculpture, for which they provided handy models. It was Le Marchand and not Rysbrack, Scheemakers, Cheere or Roubiliac who established the 'standard image' in three dimensions of several 'British Worthies' of his day, notably of Newton and Locke (Cats 68, 69). His portrait medallions were equally influential on later medallists, witness his likenesses of Stukeley and Wren (Cats 54, 48).

His wide repertory also endeared him later in the eighteenth century to an entrepreneur in the mass-production of portraits for the commercial market, Josiah Wedgwood, who evidently acquired at first or second hand casts from his ivory medallions in order to reproduce them in his novel technique of ceramic bicolour cameos. Not all proved to be popular enough to use, but Wedgwood's perspicacity has at least had the benefit of preserving an accurate record in three dimensions of some of Le Marchand's works the originals of which have since been lost, and this has aided the reconstruction of his *oeuvre* attempted in the following catalogue raisonné.

The Rediscovery of
Le Marchand's *Oeuvre*

The first 'literary', as distinct from 'documentary', record of David Le Marchand is a note penned by the Reverend Dr William Stukeley, '11 July 1722 – I sat to Mr Marchand cutting my Profile in basso rilievo in Ivory'.[1] This was the carver's last datable medallion (Cat.54), and only some four years later, in June 1726, Stukeley noted the death of his intimate friend in London, 'the famous cutter in ivory Monsr. Marchand, who cut my profile'.

George Vertue, writing from personal knowledge and observation, virtually within Le Marchand's lifetime, put his reader on notice that the carver had 'done a vast number of heads from ye life in basso relief some statues in Ivory'.[2] In his *Anecdotes of Painting in England* of 1763 Horace Walpole mentioned five of these portraits, specifying the subjects of four: a self-portrait by Le Marchand, owned by Mr (James?) West; Lord Somers; Sir Isaac Newton and Charles Marbury.[3] Then, in 1765, David's work was enshrined, before it fell into obscurity, in the newly founded British Museum, through a gift of his marvellous bust of Newton and a (less impressive) medallion of Wren (Cats 67-8) from one of the founders, Mathew Raper III FRS. Raper had a high regard for the carver, ever after his own image had been carved at the age of fifteen in 1720 (Cat.64). By an irony, this later came into the hands not of the British Museum but of the Victoria & Albert Museum, nearly two centuries later, in 1959.

However, by 1857, a French scholar writing on ivories, while republishing Walpole's short-list, bewailed the fact that 'Nous n'avons sous les yeux aucun ouvrage de cet excellent ivoirier'.[4] He reported a probable family relationship with the Guillaume Le Marchand who signed several religious paintings in St-Rémy, Dieppe. Two decades later a dictionary of French artists who worked abroad reverted to Walpole's short-list, placing David's work in England in the reign of King William III.[5] A decade later still, in 1885, a French guide for collectors of ivory repeated this information, carelessly substituting the reign of Edward III![6]

Nothing substantial was added by Lami in his *Dictionnaire des sculpteurs de l'école française sous le règne de Louis XIV* of 1906,[7] save that he reported that 'un petit bas-relief en ivoire, représentant l'Adoration des Mages, signé Le Marchand . . . se trouvait chez un antiquaire du quai Voltaire'. This signed plaque has never resurfaced, but perhaps dated from the carver's earliest days of activity in his native Dieppe: it may have resembled similar scenes by German carvers,[8] though its style would have been closer to that manifest in Le Marchand's *Miracle of Christ healing the Man with the Withered Hand* (Cat.66).

In the same year there appeared as a book in Paris a series of authoritative and well-researched articles on the ivory craftsmen of Dieppe by Ambroise Milet, Conservateur des Musées et de la Bibliothèque de la Ville de Dieppe, that had been published in the periodical *L'Art* during 1905.[9] Milet established David's date of birth as 12 October 1674, and the name of his father as Guillaume, who had married Madeleine Levasseur on 29 July 1658.

In England, meanwhile, Le Marchand's name was gradually becoming better known and associated with an ever lengthening list of subjects.

An ivory 'Bust of Rigaud' stated to be by him, and therefore probably signed, was exhibited by Mr Alfred Morrison, along with another bust of Locke, eight inches high, but not given to Le Marchand, in a prestigious exhibition of the Burlington Fine Arts Club in 1879.[10] A quarter of a century passed before Maskell pronounced in his general book of 1905 on ivories, 'Medallion portraits were a speciality of Le Marchand, and his handling of them is, in general, broad and artistic'.[11]

Two years later, but from a different point of view, the estimable L. Forrer included Le Marchand in his *Biographical Dictionary of Medallists*.[12] Shortly thereafter, Dalton catalogued professionally and illustrated Le Marchand's works in the British Museum, and so he can finally be said to have been 'put on the map' in terms of the history of art.[13] This was by then a substantial holding, for six further items, including a head of Pepys, had been given to the museum by that gifted connoisseur, the Keeper of Mediaeval and Later Antiquities, Sir Augustus Woolaston Franks KCB, between 1882 and 1895, thus generously supplementing the early gift by Mathew Raper.

The influential German writer on ivories, Christian Scherer, in an undated book of around 1905 on ivory carving since the Renaissance, was the first to draw attention to and illustrate the medallion of King George I in the Herzog Anton Ulrich-Museum in Braunschweig, which he was to catalogue fully in 1931 (Cat.34).[14] Scherer qualified Le Marchand's work as 'extraordinarily rare' and praised him as a portraitist of 'feinem Geschmack' who 'understood how to unite truth and lifelikeness in appearance with elegance and worthiness', astutely comparing his portraiture with that of the painter Rigaud. Scherer made a few further advances in an entry of 1929 in Thieme's and Becker's *Lexikon der bildenden Künstler*.[15] The signed bust of Newton and medallion of Pepys in the British Museum were singled out from among others, along with the probably early plaque of an anonymous gentleman in a banyan in Stockholm (Cat.19); and the bust of Lady Anne Churchill, Countess of Sunderland, that had been exhibited at the Burlington Fine Arts Club in London in 1923 (now Victoria & Albert Museum; Cat.25). That exhibition, dedicated solely to ivories, had naturally included several works by Le Marchand, some of them new discoveries, such as the miniature bust of Anne Sunderland and an impressive, full-frontal portrait head of a bluff-looking gentleman in a wig, but with open shirt-collar, who has on occasion been identified as Pepys, but is identified here as perhaps Sir John Houblon, first Governor of the Bank of England (Cat.70).[16]

The first enthusiast for Le Marchand in what may be called the 'modern' period of art history was Miss Margaret Longhurst, Assistant Keeper in the Department of Architecture and Sculpture at the Victoria & Albert Museum. Benefiting from the experience of the exhibition of 1923, she wrote three years later a survey of English ivories, summarising the status quo, enumerating a few recent discoveries, and pointing out that the bust of Lord Somers mentioned by Walpole was still missing.[17] However, her estimate of David's achievements was somewhat astringent: 'Le Marchand's style was not inspired, but he produced a considerable amount of honest, capable work'! Nevertheless, Longhurst's official position enabled her to take scholarly advantage of the practice of giving opinions on works of art to members of the public, and one owes to her intelligent intervention the taking of three excellent negatives of a splendid bust of John Locke, together with a note of its inscriptions and former ownership by the Raper family, that today constitute the sum total of our knowledge about this missing key piece in David's *oeuvre* (Cat.69).

Longhurst's eventual successor at the museum, Terence Hodgkinson, publishing in 1965 the charming plaque of young Matthew Raper III (Cat.64) acquired by the museum in 1959, estimated 'about twenty-five busts in the round or in relief are known'.[18] Hodgkinson was the first to explore the relationship between the ivory carver and this particularly important family of patrons, and noted the identity of Le Marchand in Highmore's portrait (see front cover and detail: ill.p.21). A similar number was cited by Simon Houfe in his pioneering article about the question of Le Marchand's patrons, whom he correctly opined were generally of the Whig persuasion.[19] John Kerslake of the National Portrait Gallery next explored further the ramifications of the Raper family, their particular support of Le Marchand and the portrait of him that they seem to have commissioned along with two portraits of themselves from Highmore (ill.pp.20-1).[20]

The present writer's interest in Le Marchand was stimulated by the three scholarly articles just mentioned, as well as by the purchase by the Victoria & Albert Museum of the superb portrait initialled D.L.M. and dated 1700 showing a young boy, Charles Chester Eyre, with a sinister coffin-shape scratched in its reverse, perhaps denoting a tragically early demise (Cat.75). A presumed filial relationship with a medallion in the Fitzwilliam Museum, Cambridge, showing one Elizabeth Eyre, that was signed in the same year stimulated further research (Cat.73). This finally bore fruit in an unexpected quarter some fifteen years later when in the deposits of the Wedgwood Museum, Barlaston, among a number of old plaster moulds and wax casts from them, wax plaques of Charles Chester Eyre and Elizabeth were identified, together with a damaged one of a gentleman clad in Roman armour within a similar, somewhat unusual, border and facing in the opposite direction to that of Elizabeth, who, it is here suggested, *may* represent her husband Charles Nicholas Eyre, as portrayed by Le Marchand in a lost ivory plaque (Cat.74).

From the 'twenty-five or so' medallions and statuettes that were known around 1970, the tally has increased continuously and considerably, partly owing to a significant rise in the value of such works of 'decorative art' in the London art market, followed by a deliberate search on all sides for examples of Le Marchand's work. With their increase in status and 'availability', an important private collection, rivalling those of the British and Victoria & Albert Museums, was amassed by Lord Thomson of Fleet, who generously agreed to lend to the exhibition of 1996 eight principal and documentary masterpieces from his yet more extensive holding.

In 1974, it was announced that a fine group of the *Virgin and Child* had been identified in the United States (Cat.92),[21] while in the following year, I had the good fortune to recognise the portrait profile of Stukeley that he himself had recorded in 1722 (Cat.54): though unsigned, it bears the subject's name inscribed on its reverse in Le Marchand's idiosyncratically childish script.[22] By 1984, about the time of the Huguenot centenary exhibition, my attention was drawn to the fact that the earliest documentary record of Le Marchand's career in this country, the permission to carve and sell ivories in Edinburgh of 1696, had been published as long before as 1962 (ill.p.14).[23] I was able to estimate the then known *oeuvre* at 'some sixty pieces', and to suggest that a medallion that had passed through Christie's in 1969, but is presently untraced, might be the self-portrait facing to the left, as recorded by Vertue.[24] Since then nine examples from David's earliest phase of activity in Edinburgh, one of them actually dated 1696, have come to light in two Scottish ancestral noble collections (Cats 6-14).

The tally of autograph works in ivory at the time of writing stands at eighty, including the three items known only from photographs, and the long lost *Adoration of the Magi*. To this figure about a dozen pieces may be added, for their previous, if not present, existence may be inferred from the three-dimensional images that survive in the Wedgwood archive of moulds or elsewhere. The sum total of David Le Marchand's known *oeuvre* is thus just over ninety items, perhaps the majority of his lifetime's output, that was qualified by Vertue as 'a vast number'.[25]

Notes to **'Le Marchand's Career'**
(pages 13-18)

1 Milet, 1905, p.210. The witnesses included another Le Marchand with an initial D. (perhaps for David, and after whom our hero may have been named). He was presumably Guillaume's father, uncle or brother, and drew a holy water stoup surmounted by a cross: this is the sort of item that was sometimes carved in ivory at Dieppe. Other members of the family followed their signatures with the signs of the human ear, or of an eye

2 One of *The Guardian Angel* in the same church is dated 1706, and another of *The Crucifixion*, removed to the museum for safety, is dated 1703, and so these are likely to be by Guillaume II, as is a *Portrait of a Lady*, wearing a red dress and a veil, dated 1701 and also in the museum. The dates after the turn of the 17th century on the latter three pictures suggest that Guillaume II at least must have converted to Catholicism, in order to be able to continue to practise his craft.

   I am grateful to Monsieur Pierre Bazin, Conservateur du Musée de Dieppe, for his help over viewing and assessing these paintings, most of which are in poor condition, owing to the aftermath of the Second World War. For practical reasons it was not possible properly to examine the pictures in St Jacques showing *The Visitation, The Finding of the True Cross* and *The Dream of Constantine*

3 It could have been carved from life only if David had indeed come many years earlier to Scotland than is documented, shortly after the Revocation of 1685 and before 1688 when the King fled into exile. However, it is scarcely credible that this maturely rendered portrait is the work of a fourteen-year-old, and it is more likely to have been derived from a medallic likeness of the sort that were struck around the time of the Glorious Revolution

4 He shares these idiosyncracies with another, less well known contemporary carver, Jean-Baptiste Basset from St-Claude in Franche-Comté, who carved at Livorno on 2 March 1696 a bust of *Cosimo III de'Medici, Grand-Duke of Tuscany* (ill.p.26); Philippovich Collection, Vienna; see Philippovich, 1982, pp.87-9, figs 66-7)

5 J. Edleston, *Correspondence of Sir Isaac Newton and Professor Cotes, including letters of other eminent men . . .*, London, 1850, p.LXXXI. For the 'bust' owned by Newton recorded in his posthumous inventory, see Gjertsen, 1986, p.445 – 'a figure cut in ivory of Sir Isaac in a glass frame'. This wording makes it sound more like a relief, and the use of the word figure means that it may have been the half-length relief that came later into the possession of Dr Mead (Cat.44) or the lost one (Cat.46).

   Gjertsen's items 4-5 have been personally examined by the present writer and are not by Le Marchand (nor probably by Van der Hagen, to whom they have previously been attributed, for their style is too 'waxy' and not incisive enough); while his no.3 is apparently no longer in King's College, Cambridge, to which it was supposedly 'presented' by Keynes. One wonders if they might be by a contemporary carver such as Mathieu Gosset, whose *œuvre* remains to be explored

6 P. Earle, *The Making of the English Middle Class: Business, Society and Family Life in London 1610-1730*, London, 1991

7 Houfe, 1971

8 For this and the following references see: *Publications of the Huguenot Society* ('Quarto series'), XXVII (1923), p.85; XXVIII (1924), p.22; XXIX (1926), pp.90, 107, 117; LIII (1977), *s.v.* Le Marchant

9 E. J. Pyke, *A Biographical Dictionary of Wax Modellers*, Oxford, 1973, p.59; Vertue, III, pp.160-1, writing on his better-known nephew Isaac, a prolific mid-18th century modeller of portrait miniatures in wax, described Mathieu as, 'much esteemed for his works, casting in wax all sorts of small figures – from Ivory-carvings – antient and modern, statues, Busts, medallions &c. by which he gained a considerable fortune and dyd rich'. Among the items described by Vertue as 'modern' may have been some by Le Marchand

Notes to **'Le Marchand, the Raper Family and the Early Bank of England'**
(pages 19-25)

1 Hodgkinson, 1965, and Kerslake, 1972. I am greatly indebted to both articles, and to their authors, for subsequent discussions of Le Marchand problems

2 Minor amendments have been incorporated, gleaned from the records of Directors of the Bank of England

3 They represent: *The Good Samaritan* and *Christ healing the Palsied Man*

4 Moses' description of himself as 'Junior' also indicates a forebear of the same name, who remains to be tracked down eventually

5 P. Earle, *The Making of the English Middle Class: Business, Society and Family life in London 1610-1730*, London, 1991

6 Moses was Director in 1716-19, 1720-3, 1724-6, 1727-30, 1731-4, 1735-8 and 1732-42; while Mathew II was in 1730-3, 1734-6, 1737-40, 1741-4, 1745-6, and from 1747 until his death in 1748. Neither aspired to the more prestigious, yet perhaps more time-consuming – and not necessarily more remunerative – offices of Governor or Deputy, perhaps on account of their other business commitments

7 J. Giuseppi, *The Bank of England*, London, 1966, p.14

8 I am grateful to Mr John Keyworth, Curator of the Bank of England Museum, for his kindness in showing me the painted portraits of the early Directors, allowing me access to the Bank's records of their Directorships, supplying me with relevant photographs and granting permission to reproduce them here

9 Dame Alice Archer Houblon, *The Houblon Family, its story and times*, London, 1907

10 Bank of England Archive, COU. No.B367/3, unpublished, selective, typescript entitled: *The Morice Letters, 1701-1731: A collection of letters written by Humphry Morice, sometime Governor of the Bank of England*, ed. W. Marston Acres FRHS, pp.58-9, no.109. Also in complete typescript by the same editor, *Transcript of Letters 1701-31 addressed to Humphrey Morice* [COU. No.B151/3], pp.727-8, no.508

11 *Morice Letters*, pp.124-5, no.249; *Transcript*, pp.735-6, no.515

12 *Transcript*, pp.738-9, no.516

Note to **'The Art of Ivory Carving'**
(pages 25-27)

1 Philippovich, 1961/82, p.87, figs 66-7: my thanks to Herrn Dr von Philippovich of Vienna for kindly providing photographs of the latter, which he owns, and permitting them to be reproduced again here

1 W. C. Lukis (ed.), *Family Memoirs of Stukeley* (Surtees Society), London, 1882, I,
pp.67, 131, n.26

2 Vertue, III, p.13

3 *Walpole* (ed. R. N. Wornum), 1849, II, p.625

4 Chennevières-Pointel, 1857, p.12

5 Dussieux, 1876, p.273

6 Maze-Sencier, 1885, p.639

7 Lami, 1906, p.317

8 R. Berliner, *Die Bildwerke des Bayerischen Nationalmuseums, IV. Abteilung: Die Bildwerke
in Elfenbein . . .*, Augsburg, 1926, nos 411, 882

9 Milet, 1905, pp.31-5; 161-7; 209-17; 309f.; 405-13. See esp. pp.210-11 for Le
Marchand. Published as a book in Paris, 1906

10 Burlington Fine Arts Club, *Catalogue of Bronzes and Ivories of European Origin,
exhibited in 1879*, London, 1879, nos 73 and 70 respectively, but neither
unfortunately illustrated [an exhibition not to be confused with the later and more
important one devoted to ivories alone, held in 1923, see Bibliography].
    Mr Morrison's bust identified as 'Locke, 8 in high', is the right height to have
been one of Le Marchand's images, but was not recorded as having been signed,
and is therefore unlikely to have been the now lost prime version (Cat.69); if it
was the third version, that bears Locke's name alone on its verso (Cat.69c), or
indeed the second, uninscribed version (Cat.69a), it seems odd that it was
exhibited without one of the pendant busts of Newton with which both the latter
were paired when they first appeared on the art market in 1953 and 1965
respectively

11 Maskell, 1905, pp.385-7, pl.66

12 London, III, 1907, p.390: 'Le Merchant. Carver of Portrait-medallions in ivory,
who flourished in the second half of the seventeenth century'; *Supplement*, VII,
1927, p.547, he listed inaccurately in the British Museum, alongside Pepys and
Wren, an image of the Duke of Cumberland, which is in fact by Cavalier

13 Dalton, 1909, pp.151-2, nos 455-62, pls CI, CIII, CVIII

14 Scherer, *c.*1905, pp.25-6, fig.19: 'Marchand zeigt sich in diesem Werk als ein
Porträtist von feinem Geschmack, der Wahrheit und Lebendigkeit des Ausdrucks
mit Eleganz und Würde geschickt zu vereinigen versteht und hierin geradezu mit
Rigaud verglichen werden kann, an dessen Bildnisse seine Werke lebhaft
erinnern'. See also, Scherer, 1931, p.110, no.351, pl.54

15 Thieme and Becker, 1929, XXIII, p.20

16 BFAC, 1923, nos 219, 221, pl.LII, etc.

17 Longhurst, 1926, pp.59-60

18 Hodgkinson, 1965, p.29

19 Houfe, 1971, p.66

20 Kerslake, 1972, p.25f.

21 Foah, 1974, pp.38-43

22 Avery, 1985, p.1564, fig.7

23 H. Armet (ed.), *Extracts from the records of the Burgh of Edinburgh*, Edinburgh/
London, 1962, p.189 and Introduction, p.xxviii: this was drawn to my attention by
Dr Gwynn, Director of Huguenot Heritage

24 Avery, 1984

25 Of these, owing to restrictions of funding that precluded all but a few loans from
abroad, just over sixty actual ivory carvings were included in the exhibition of
1996, alongside all the items from Wedgwood that bear witness to the existence
of lost images in ivory. The absent remainder are however included in the present
catalogue raisonné in their logical position and in numerical sequence

PLATE I
David Le Marchand, *Sir Humphry Morice, Governor of
the Bank of England? (1679-1731)*, 1716-20 (Cat.71)

PLATE 2
David Le Marchand, *Francis Sambrooke (b.1662)*,
1704 (Cat.58)

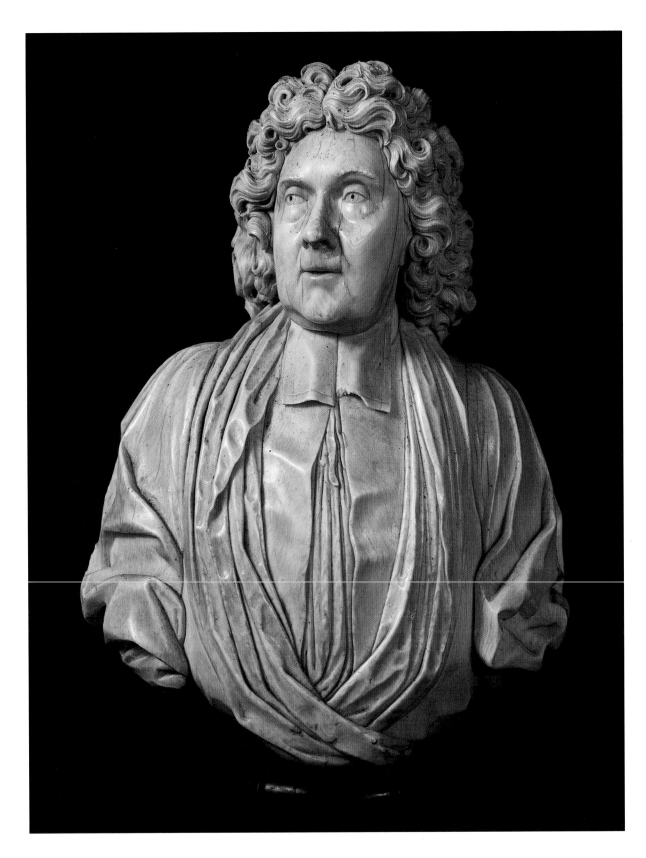

PLATE 3
David Le Marchand, *John Vesey, Archbishop of Tuam*
(1638-1716), 1702 (Cat.38)

PLATE 4
David Le Marchand, *Matthew Raper III FRS*
(1704-1778), 1720 (Cat.64)

PLATE 5
David Le Marchand, *Noblewoman sitting with her daughter and a pet whippet* (perhaps Anne, Countess of Sunderland, with her daughter Anne, later Viscountess Bateman), *c.*1710 (Cat.28)

PLATE 6
David Le Marchand,
Crucified Christ (Cat.93)

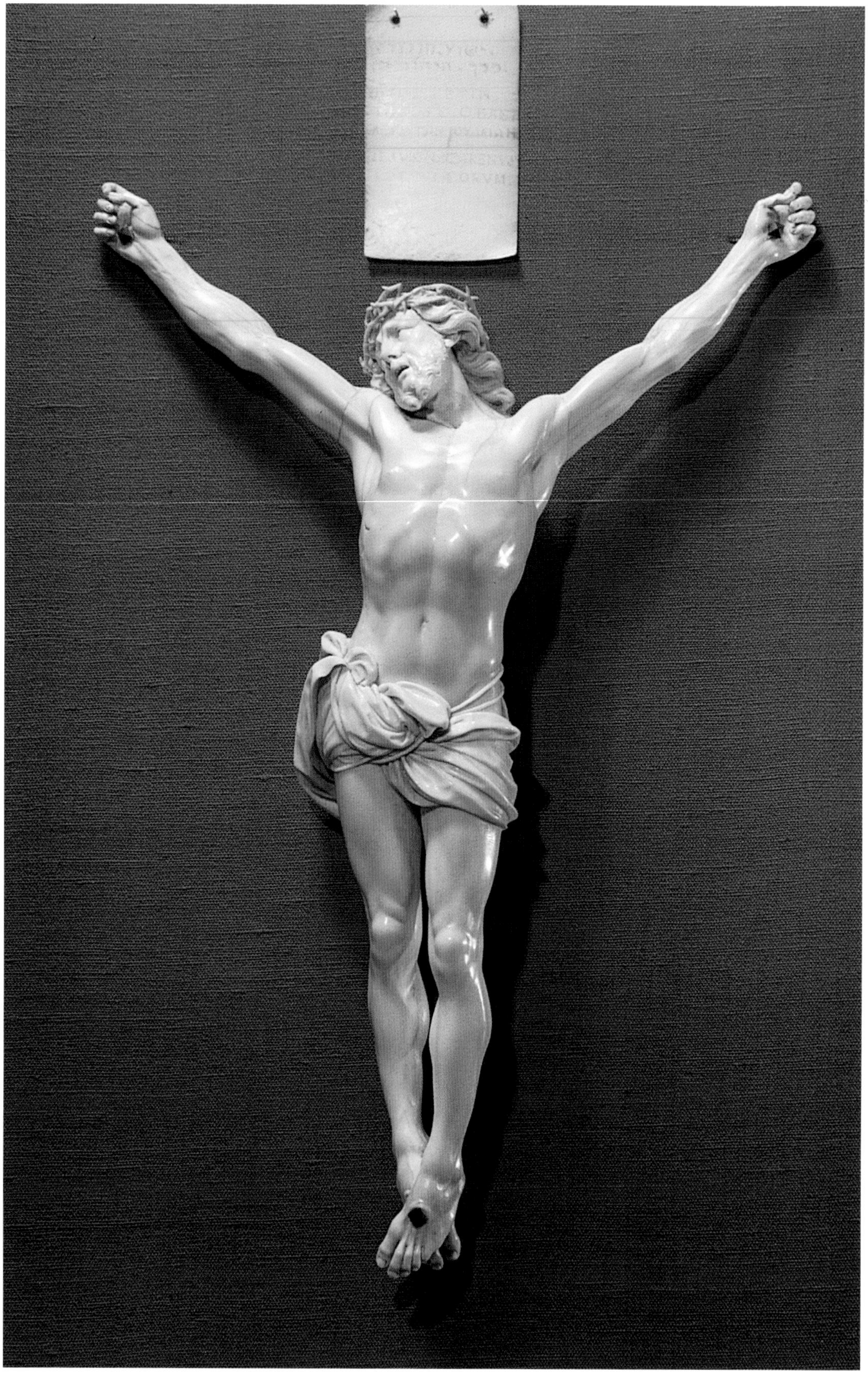

PLATE 7
David Le Marchand,
Venus and Cupid, 1710-20 (Cat.95)

PLATE 8
David Le Marchand, *Sir John Houblon, Lord Mayor of London (1632-1712?)*, c.1710 (Cat.70)

PLATE 10
David Le Marchand, *Sir Isaac Newton, PRS*
(1642-1727), 1714 (Cat.47)

PLATE II
David Le Marchand, *John Locke (1632-1704)*, *c.*1718?, lost
(Cat.69)

PLATE 12
David Le Marchand, *Samuel Pepys (1633-1703)*, 1700-05 (Cat.40)

PLATE 13
David Le Marchand, *Queen Anne (1665-1714)*, 1702-12 (Cat.20)

PLATE 14
David Le Marchand, *Sir Isaac Newton, PRS*
(1642-1727), 1702-10 (Cat.44)

PLATE 15
David Le Marchand (after a wax model, perhaps by
François Le Pipre), *Thomas Guy (1645-1724)*, 1700-26 (Cat.42)

PLATE 16
David Le Marchand, *Anonymous Nobleman* (possibly
Louis, Dauphin of France, *d*.1711), 1700 (Cat.29)

Catalogue

NOTE

Dimensions are given in the following order:
cm (in); height, width, depth

Books and articles appearing in the Bibliography (p.110) are abbreviated; those not in the Bibliography are given in full

Works appearing in the British Museum's 1996 touring exhibition are indicated by an asterisk after their catalogue number

All works are illustrated alongside their catalogue entry, except where they appear in the plate section between pages 33 and 48, and Cat.61, which appears on page 1

Le Marchand's Beginnings in Dieppe, and his French Subjects

David Le Marchand learned his craft in his native town of Dieppe, the French port to which elephant tusks had been shipped from West Africa, possibly since the late Middle Ages, and which therefore became a major centre for ivory working. Alongside artistic carving of images, both religious and secular, the craft of turning ivory on lathes, frequently complex, eccentric ones which achieved amazing abstract geometrical shapes, flourished, as well as the production of humbler – and often amusingly decorated – domestic artefacts such as combs, tobacco-rasps, snuff-box and counter-box tops. Dozens of families were engaged in producing or marketing these wares and the Dieppois even had a warehouse in Paris to further their enterprises.

However, David's father Guillaume was a painter, several of whose altarpieces survive in the churches and museum of Dieppe. The Le Marchands, who were Huguenot Protestants, were affected, while David was still a child, by religious persecution in France after the Revocation in 1685 of the Edict of Nantes (which had since the late sixteenth century guaranteed freedom of faith). While some families converted expediently to Catholicism, one hundred and forty of them fled. Dieppe was virtually razed to the ground by a bombardment of the Anglo-Dutch fleet in 1694, but even that catastrophe did not destroy the civic tradition of working ivory and it survived well into the nineteenth, and even the early twentieth century.

What may be David le Marchand's earliest portrait, dated 1689, is still in France (Dieppe Museum), while he also portrayed King Louis XIV, presumably before leaving his native land. He also copied brilliantly in ivory an allegorical marble statue by Regnaudin in the gardens of Versailles, and it seems likely that he saw it for himself, for its design is very complex, and so would be hard to reconstruct from a two-dimensional image, such as the engraving in Thomassin's illustrated book *Recueil des Figures. Statues de Versailles*, printed in Paris 1694 (pl.77).

1

Sebastien Le Prestre, Maréchal de Vauban (1633-1707)? 1689
Portrait medallion; three-quarter face to right
8×6 ($3\frac{1}{8} \times 2\frac{3}{8}$)
Château Musée de Dieppe [987.1.1]
Condition: carved in relatively deep relief on a thick, octagonal plaque
Inscr: .LE.MARCHAND.FECIT./ ANNO 1689

PROV: G. Holville, Paris (until 1987)

This unpublished portrait plaque turned up in the art trade in France in 1987 and after its export had been blocked was purchased for the museum in Dieppe. It was thus reasonable to infer that the sitter was French, rather than British.

It has been suggested by M. Pierre Bazin, Curator of the Château

Musée de Dieppe, that the subject may instead be King Louis' successful general, a genius at siege warfare and the use of artillery, the Maréchal de Vauban. Bazin points to a comparison with, *eg* a portrait of Vauban painted by Rigaud, where the wig is similarly tied up appropriately for military action (Couturier Nicolay, Drouôt, Paris, sale 27 June 1980, lot 89). Nevertheless, it does not correspond particularly well with the later bust by Coysevox of 1704-6 (F. Souchal, *French Sculptors of the 17th and 18th centuries: The reign of Louis XIV*, Oxford, 1977, I, pp.211-12, no.82).

The signature does not specify whether this portrait is by David, or some other member of the family. If it is by him, it is his earliest dated work, carved when he was only fifteen years old, perhaps still an apprentice. This may account for some slightly gauche features, notably in the relationship of the turned head to the shoulder, with its prominent lion's mask paldron, and the failure to establish convincingly the position of the cuirass beneath the cloak as it runs across the chest.

However, the military image conveyed by the imperious turn of the head and firmly jutting chin, with clenched lips, is analogous with that of his miniature bust of the 2nd Earl of Cromartie (Cat.7), carved probably some seven or eight years later. Furthermore, the treatment of the curls of the wig, with the bottom tied in a knot, may be paralleled in the bust of the Earl, and his later full-face plaques of Thomas Guy and Newton (Cats 42, 44).

1

The epigraphy of the inscription, with its well-formed italic capitals and neat serifs, is unlike that on most of David's later reliefs, which is bolder and less tidy, but the discrepancy may also be between an apprentice's nervous accuracy, and the bravura of a mature artist. All of the signatures or initials on his early carvings in Scotland are neatly executed, though not as prettily as here.

It must be admitted that the mere fact that the plaque turned up in France does not necessarily mean, particularly in these days of an aggressively international art trade, that it was carved there. Such an easily portable item *could* have been moved anywhere, either long ago or more recently. However, if the assumptions above *are* in order, they indicate that David was perhaps still in France, if not in Dieppe, and that his father Guillaume may *not* have fled abroad with his family immediately after the Revocation of the Edict of Nantes in 1685, as has generally been assumed. In that case, David may not have arrived in Great Britain long before he set up shop in Edinburgh in 1696.

If the assumptions are wrong, then this item, if indeed by David, may not represent Vauban or any other Frenchman and may have been carved when he was already in exile, possibly in England or in Scotland. In any case, in terms of style it fits in rather well with the carvings that he executed in 1696 or shortly thereafter in Edinburgh, and makes a convincing addition to his *oeuvre*, as his début into the art world.

2

**2*

King Louis XIV (1638-1715)** *c.*1695-6
Portrait medallion; profile to the right
8.5×7.1 $\left(3\frac{3}{8} \times 2\frac{13}{16}\right)$
Simon Houfe Esq.
Condition: good
Inscr: D.L.M.F.

PROV: Art Trade, Edinburgh (bought by Lady Richardson, *c.*1941, £5)

LIT: Houfe, 1971, p.67, fig.2; Houfe, 1980, p.152

The provenance from Edinburgh, the grand, French subject and the low-relief point to a date early in Le Marchand's career. This may be either a specimen of his carving made in France, that he brought with him to Edinburgh in 1696 to display his talents, or an item made just after then, for some Jacobite who went into exile to St-Germain with King James II & VII, where the Sun King was their host.

Houfe (1980) tells of its acquisition by Lady Richardson.

3* (Plate 9)
After Thomas Regnaudin (1622-1706)
Saturn Abducting Cybele (or 'Time Revealing Truth', or 'Time with Opportunity and Penitence') 1700-20
Ivory sculpture
Height (to the hand holding the forelock): 20.3 (8)
Height (to the top of the arrow): 23.7 $\left(9\frac{5}{16}\right)$
The Victoria & Albert Museum, London, A.1-1935
Condition: excellent; arrow now lost
Inscr: (on the surface of the base, behind the lion's tail) D.L.M.Sc.

3

PROV: Given by Dr W. L. Hildburgh

LIT: The Victoria & Albert Museum, *Review*, 1935, p.7, fig.4;
R. Wittkower, 'Chance, Time and Virtue', in *Journal of the Warburg &
Courtauld Institutes*, I, no.4, 1937-8, pp.315ff., pl.49; M. Lidstone, 'The
Hildburgh Treasures', in *The Antique Collector*, April 1958, repr.;
Whinney, 1971, p.28, no.2;
F. Souchal, *French Sculptors of the 17th and 18th centuries: The reign of
Louis XIV*, III, Oxford, 1987, pp.250-1

The composition reflects the artist's native background, for it is reduced
from a monumental marble group by Regnaudin for the gardens of
Versailles (1675-87: now in the Louvre). It was designed by Charles Le
Brun (whose drawings survive in the Albertina, Vienna) as one of a set of
four depicting mythological abductions for the Parterre d'Eau. The
figure below represents Ceres, anguished at the event.

Confusion over the subject as represented by Le Marchand was caused
only because Regnaudin subsequently exhibited in the Paris Salon of
1699 a model entitled 'Time Revealing Truth'. As that model is lost, one
cannot tell whether it was identical in composition to the marble group,
or a variation. The new subject has given rise to much scholarly
speculation: Wittkower (*loc.cit.*) regarded this ivory as a representation of
'Missed Opportunity', *ie* Opportunity seized by Time takes her own
forelock and kills herself. The woman with the lion he regarded as
representing Penitence or Regret.

As Margaret Whinney perceptively wrote, 'Apart from the fascination
of its complex subject, it is not surprising that the group, with its
intricate spiral composition, attracted the attention of sculptors working
on a small scale, for it gives considerable opportunity for a display of
virtuosity, a quality much prized in the early eighteenth century.' The
sheer brilliance of reducing the original monumental group to such a
small scale, while retaining its vigour and clarity, and the cunning with
which it is carved out of a single tusk without additions sets Le
Marchand in the top rank of European ivory sculptors of all time.

Versions of Regnaudin's spectacular composition were carved
elsewhere in Europe, for instance by J. Dobberman in amber (Kassel,
Hessisches Landesmuseum),[1] and by Joachim Henne, in ivory, *c.*1673
(Copenhagen, National Museum, D.368),[2] the latter capturing the
spiralling movement of the original rather better than Le Marchand did,
for he has turned the main figures into a frontal plane. A later version in
pipe-clay, perhaps Flemish or Northern French, from the circle of Paul-
Louis Cifflé (1724-1806),[3] was modelled in reverse, which suggests that it
was derived from an engraving, the most easily accessible of which was
in Thomassin, *Recueil des Figures. Statues de Versailles* (Paris, 1694, pl.77:
captioned '*Le Temps, et l'Occasion*').

This impressive technical achievement points to a date towards the
middle or end of Le Marchand's career, but it is grouped here with his
early, French period in view of its subject.

1 A. Rohde, *Bernstein*, Berlin, 1937, 59, no.237, pl.93
2 C. Theuerkauff, 'Jacob Dobbermann und Joachim Hennen – Anmerkungen zu einigen
  Kleinbildwerken', in *Alte und Moderne Kunst*, XXIV, 162, 1979, pp.16-26, pl.31
3 With Michael Hall Fine Arts Inc, New York, 1979; this or a similar item sold Sotheby's,
  New York, 22 June 1989, lot 206A

Beginnings in Edinburgh (1696-99?): Scottish Patrons

David le Marchand was first recorded in the United Kingdom in 1696,
when on 12 February he was given permission by the city fathers of
Edinburgh to open a shop, on condition that he took on Scottish
children as apprentices: his choice of Edinburgh was perhaps due to the
Auld Alliance between Scotland and France, and he joined a colony of
Huguenots in the city. The fact that Le Marchand began his career in
Scotland is a relatively recent, exciting and unexpected discovery, for it
had always been assumed that he had started in London, where he
resided and worked later: however, nine recently discovered ivories from
noble Scottish collections attest to his presence and diligent activity for
Scottish noble patrons, alongside a pair that was already known showing
the Earl and Countess of Leven.

Le Marchand may already have made before 1696 (when he was aged
twenty-four) a few carvings in France and perhaps some in Scotland, for
there exist a counter-box top recording the Birth of Prince James ('The
Old Pretender') in 1688 and a portrait medallion showing King James II
& VII, which resembles his appearance on a medal recording his flight to
France in 1689: however, both may have been made slightly later for
Jacobites.

Le Marchand carved and dated in 1696, the year he opened his shop
in Edinburgh, a portrait of James Mackenzie (later Lord Royston) and
this was probably when he also carved his father, George, 1st Earl of
Cromartie and a small bust of his brother, the 2nd Earl, as well as two
others of their relations, all of which are still in the possession of their
descendants. Another fascinating recent discovery is a series of ivories in
Drummond Castle, a pair showing James, 2nd titular Duke, and his
Duchess, as well as a disc with the Drummond/Perth coat-of-arms, with
the Order of the Thistle displayed, and the portrait of King James II &
VII. The recently immigrated ivory carver, despite his Huguenot
affiliations, was thus immediately and enthusiastically patronised by
prominent Jacobites.

4*
David Melville 3rd Earl of Leven and 2nd Earl of Melville
(1660-1728) 1696-1700
Portrait medallion; profile to the right
8.25 × 6.7 ($3\frac{1}{4} × 2\frac{5}{8}$)
The Victoria & Albert Museum, London, A.123-1956
Bequeathed by Dr W. L. Hildburgh, having been on loan since
November 1955 (No.5265)
Condition: good
INSCR: DAVID EARLE OF LEVEN

PROV: S. Hand Esq, deceased (Sotheby's, 3 November 1955, lot 9 (£10))

EXH: *Virtue and Vision: Sculpture and Scotland 1540-1990*, Royal Scottish Academy, Edinburgh, 18 July–15 September 1991, repr. p.137

LIT: J. B. Paul (ed.), *The Scots Peerage . . .*, Edinburgh, 1909, VI, pp.110-12

This portrait medallion is paired with one of the sitter's wife, Anna, Countess of Leven (Cat.5) that bears Le Marchand's initials. Their relatively simple style in shallow relief, which they share with the medallions of the Mackenzies (Cats 6, 8-10), suggests that they date from the beginning of Le Marchand's career in Edinburgh, just after 1696.

David Melville, who assumed the title of (3rd) Earl of Leven on 27 July 1681, was a military commander. Although he was not implicated in the Rye House plot, he accompanied his father, George, 1st Earl of Melville, to Holland. In 1685 he entered the service of the Elector of Brandenburg as Captain of Horse, being appointed Colonel two years later. At the court of Berlin he acted as confidential agent to the Prince of Orange. Subsequently at his own expense he raised a regiment of Scottish refugees in Germany and Holland, of which he was appointed Colonel in 1688, and with which he accompanied the Prince of Orange to England. The regiment was chosen to garrison Plymouth after its surrender.

Leven was selected by William of Orange to be the bearer of his letter to the Scottish Convention in March 1689. He was also empowered to raise a regiment of 800 men to guard Edinburgh until the arrival of regular troops from England. His own regiment subsequently arrived in Scotland and stood firm at the Battle of Killiecrankie, for which he received credit.

Leven took an active part in promoting the succession of Queen Anne in 1702 and in 1704 was restored to the command of the castle in Edinburgh and in 1706 was appointed Commander-in-Chief of the forces in Scotland. After the union he was chosen as a representative peer for Scotland and was re-elected until 1710. In 1712 he was deprived of all his offices by the Tory administration.

It is stated that 'in the beginning of his life Leven was so vain and conceity that he became the jest of all sober men', but admitted that 'as he grew older he overcame that folly in part and from the proudest became the civilest man alive'; and that he 'was a man of good parts and sound judgment', although 'master of no kind of learning'.

An interest in art was shown by David and his father, the 1st Earl of Melville, for they were largely responsible for persuading Sir John Baptist Medina to come north and to settle in Scotland. It was probably during the time when first he was Keeper of Edinburgh Castle (1689-1702) that Lord Melville was also an early patron of Le Marchand, when he set up shop in the city.

5*
Anna Countess of Leven (*c.*1675-1702) *c.*1696-1700

Portrait medallion; profile to the left
7.5 × 5.2 (3 × 2⅛)
The Victoria & Albert Museum, London, A.124-1956
Bequeathed by Dr W. L. Hildburgh, having been on loan since November 1955 (No.5266)
Condition: slightly discoloured; incipient crack at left
Inscr: ANNA COVNTESS OF LEVEN; (on the ground below the truncation of the shoulder) D.L.M.F.

PROV: S. Hand Esq, deceased (Sotheby's, 3 November 1955, lot 9 (£10))

EXH: *Virtue and Vision: Sculpture and Scotland 1540-1990*, Royal Scottish Academy, Edinburgh, 18 July–15 September 1991, repr. p.137

LIT: J. B. Paul (ed.), *The Scots Peerage . . .*, Edinburgh, 1909, VI, p.112; see also II, 1905, pp.281-3; and III, 1906, p.77

Anna was the eldest daughter of Sir James Wemyss, Lord Burntisland (*d.*1682), and Margaret, Countess of Wemyss (*d.*1705), and sister of David, 3rd Earl of Wemyss. Her parents married in 1672 and she was the third of five children, so she was presumably born *c.*1675. This portrait

4

5

medallion is paired with one of her husband, David, Earl of Leven, whom she married on 3 September 1691 (Cat.4). Their relatively simple style in shallow relief, which they share with the medallions of the Mackenzies (Cats 6, 8-10), suggests that they may date from the beginning of Le Marchand's career in Edinburgh, after 1696.

After Lord Burntisland's death in 1682, Margaret married in April 1700 Sir George Mackenzie, Viscount Tarbat, afterwards Earl of Cromartie. She died in 1705. This second marriage of hers is of interest in the present context, inasmuch as it furnishes a link between two of the most important Scottish families who patronised Le Marchand.

6*
Sir George Mackenzie, Baronet; from 1685 Viscount Tarbat; from 1703, 1st Earl of Cromartie (1630-1714) 1696-1700
Portrait medallion; profile to the right, in full wig, classical armour and cloak
8×6.5 ($3\frac{1}{2} \times 2\frac{9}{16}$)
Private Collection
Condition: good

PROV: By family descent

LIT: J. B. Paul (ed.), *The Scots Peerage . . .*, Edinburgh, 1906, III, pp.72-5; W. Fraser, *The Earls of Cromartie, their kindred, country and correspondence*, Edinburgh, 1876, 2 vols, esp. vol.I, LXVII-CXCIV (memoir of the 1st Earl)

The medallion is neither signed nor identified, but it is attributable to Le Marchand through its association in a single family collection with three other medallions, of which two are signed and a third is dated 1696 (Cats 8, 9, 10). The backing paper of the frame is inscribed with the sitter's name and eventual title. It was removed to see if the reverse of the ivory had any inscription, but there was none and the surface had been left rough.

Sir George Mackenzie was born at Innerteil in 1630 and was educated at the University of St Andrews and at King's College, Aberdeen, where

6

he graduated in 1646. He took part in Glencairn's expedition on behalf of Charles II, but after Middleton's defeat at Lochgair in 1654 escaped to the continent, where he remained until the Restoration. Thereafter he was appointed a Lord of Session in 1661, though dismissed in 1664, and a member of the Estates for Ross-shire, taking an active part in Parliament. In 1685 he received from James II & VII a grant of a further pension and was raised to the peerage as Viscount Tarbat, Lord Macleod and Castlehaven.

At the Revolution he secured his position with the new rulers and by advising in council the disbandment of the militia facilitated the establishment of King William's government. After Killiecrankie he was employed in negotiations with the Highland chiefs and in 1692 he was reinstated as Lord Clark Register. He held the office until 1696, when he retired.

On the accession of Queen Anne he became Secretary of State for Scotland and on 1 January 1703 he was advanced to the dignity of Earl of Cromartie. In May that year he became Captain General of the Royal Company of Archers. From 1705-10 he was Lord Justice General, vigorously supporting the Union of England and Scotland. His last years were spent in retirement in Ross-shire.

George Mackenzie was one of the original Fellows of the Royal Society, contributing several papers to its early *Transactions*. He also wrote many publications on political, historical and ecclesiastical subjects. His portrait by Sir John Baptist Medina is in the Scottish National Portrait Gallery and his patronage of the artist tends to link him with the Melvilles (see Cat.4). His second son John succeeded him (Cat.7), while his fourth son was James, of Royston, created a Baronet in 1704 (Cat.8).

7*
John Mackenzie, 2nd Earl of Cromartie (c.1656-1731) 1696-1700
Miniature bust
7.5 (3)
Private Collection
Condition: cracked in certain places, along the grain of the ivory, and crosswards at the neck

PROV: By family descent

LIT: J. B. Paul (ed.), *The Scots Peerage . . .*, Edinburgh, 1906, II, p.76; W. Fraser, *The Earls of Cromartie, their kindred, country and correspondence*, Edinburgh, 1876, pp.420-4

The bust is neither signed nor identified, but it is attributable to Le Marchand through its association in a single family collection with four medallions, of which two are signed and a third is dated 1696 (Cats 6, 8, 9, 10). A traditional identification as the 1st Earl has been abandoned in favour of one as the 2nd Earl, for the father is already accounted for in the series of portraits.

On his father's creation as Viscount Tarbat in 1685, John took the designation of Master of Tarbat. In May 1689 he was arrested under suspicion of hostility to William and Mary, but in December was released on parole by order of the Privy Council. In August 1691 he was tried for the murder of Elias Poiret, Sieur de la Roche, a French Protestant refugee and Gentleman of the King's Guard, killed in a scuffle in a vintner's in the Kirkgate of Leith, but was acquitted. When in 1703 his father became Earl of Cromartie, he took the courtesy title of Lord Macleod. His first wife, Lady Elizabeth Gordon (m.1685), proved a spendthrift, contracting large debts for 'meat, drink, cloaths, abulziments, rings, bracelets, and jewals of great value [sic]', and they were, not surprisingly, divorced in 1698. John's monetary affairs were much embarrassed and in 1724 the estate of Cromartie was sequestrated. He died at Castle Leod in 1731.

John Mackenzie's brush with a French Protestant grandee does not seem to have prevented him from allowing another, humbler, one to carve his portrait. This is Le Marchand's first surviving exercise in portraiture in the round, and he evidently enjoyed the freedom to carve the luxuriant curls of the full wig behind, as well as in front of, the shoulders. The grotesque mask at the centre of the cuirass was a normal apotropaic emblem, to ward off an enemy. The military image, with its commanding turn of the head and determined expression, is easy to relate to the portrait plaque perhaps showing Vauban dated 1689 (Cat.1).

8*
Sir James Mackenzie of Royston, from 1704, Baronet, Lord Royston (1671 or 74-1744) 1696
Portrait medallion, profile to the right in wig, classical armour and cloak
8.3 × 7 (4 × 2¾)
Private Collection
Condition: excellent
Inscr: (in raised capital letters) IAC.MCKENZIE / AET XXII 1696

PROV: By family descent

LIT: J. B. Paul (ed.), *The Scots Peerage . . .*, Edinburgh, 1906, II, p.76; W. Fraser, *The Earls of Cromartie, their kindred, country and correspondence*, Edinburgh, 1876, pp.420-4

The medallion is not signed, but it is attributable to Le Marchand through its association in a single family collection with three other medallions, of which two are signed (Cats 6, 9, 10). The inscribed date of 1696 corresponds exactly with the year in which the ivory carver opened his shop in Edinburgh and so this group of portraits of the Mackenzies may have been one of his earliest commissions. The careful classical epigraphy of the inscription and the fact that it is left in relief, a far more laborious technique than merely incising it, are akin to the practice of Jean Cavalier, Le Marchand's immediate predecessor.

James was the fourth son (the third to survive) of George, 1st Earl of Cromartie (Cat.6), and thus a younger brother to John, 2nd Earl (Cat.7). He is said to have been born in 1671, which is – inexplicably – discrepant with the data of the inscription. He studied at the University of Oxford, where he was a diligent student, for his Professor wrote to his lawyer father on 25 March 1693, 'I may advise your Lordship that his whole conduct at Oxon has been such as your Lordship would have approved every step of it hade you been present'. Indeed, James's serious application to his studies even incurred the dislike of some of his fellow undergraduates at Oxford, for they were jealous of his potential success.

William Strachan, according to Fraser (*op.cit.*), also wrote six months later, 'He has spent his time very diligently in his studies, and the daily improvements that he makes therein do give just grounds to hope that he will prove a comfort to his relations, and an ornament to his country. His civil and prudent carriage has recommended him very much to the favour and good esteem of Dr Bouchier, of our professor of law, Dr Charlet, and several other persons of considerable note in this university. I am only sorry that we are so soon to be deprived of his company, for this day he parted from hence on his journey to Holland.' This was in order to pursue his studies in the University of Utrecht, which was much favoured by the Scots at the time, with fifty of them studying there, according to a letter from James, who also found the cost of living not as cheap as at Oxford.

On completing his education, he devoted himself to the profession of Law, was admitted Advocate on 19 November 1698, and soon became one of the most distinguished members of the Scottish Bar. Queen Anne created him a Baronet in 1704, in recognition of his and his father's

7

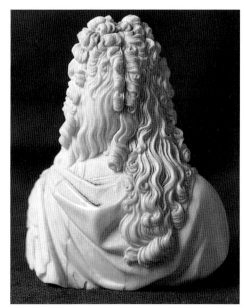

7

services to her and her forebears. He married Elizabeth, the widowed youngest daughter of Sir George Mackenzie of Rosehaugh, well known as Lord Advocate in the reigns of Charles II and James II & VII, who, owing to the severity with which he prosecuted Non-conformists, became known among the Covenanters as 'bloody Mackenzie'.

The present portrait, if – as is likely – it was taken from life, must have been carved during a vacation from the University of Utrecht. Otherwise, Le Marchand could have made use of a profile portrait sketched by some artist in Holland. Despite his youth and scholarly inclination for the Law, James is shown, as was customary for noblemen, in classical armour. There is a deliberate likeness between his image and that of his father (Cat.6), emphasised by the fact that both profiles face the same direction, but James's head is smaller, as though to indicate his youth. His mother, Anna (d.1699), was perhaps carved at the same time, and her profile would naturally have been contrived to make a facing pair with that of her husband.

9*
Lady Mackenzie of Rosehaugh, née Margaret Haliburton
(c.1654-1713) 1696-1700
Portrait medallion; profile to the left, in décolleté dress with her hair up and bound with a string of pearls, as is the shoulder of her dress
8×6.5 ($3\frac{1}{8} \times 2\frac{9}{16}$)
Private Collection
Condition: very fine
Inscr: (round the upper rim, partly hidden by the frame) D. MARGARAT HALIBVRTON, AET XLII; (on the ground below the truncation) D.L.MD.F.

PROV: By family descent

LIT: W. Fraser, *The Earls of Cromartie, their kindred, country and correspondence*, Edinburgh, 1876, pp.72-3

Daughter of the Laird of Pitcur, Margaret married Sir George Mackenzie of Rosehaugh (1636-91; for whom see Cat.8). By her first marriage,

Margaret had a son, George Mackenzie of Rosehaugh, with whose portrait as a ten-year-old this medallion forms a facing pair (Cat.10), probably in view of her husband's demise a few years earlier. Some time after 1700 Margaret married Roderick, Lord Prestonhall, when Mary, his first wife died. Roderick was the middle son of the 1st Earl of Cromartie and so by this second marriage, Margaret became sister-in-law of the 1st Earl (Cat.6) towards the end of his life, and an aunt of the 2nd Earl (Cat.7).

Le Marchand conveys admirably an impression of a forceful, well-endowed forty-two-year-old widow, who was probably determined to do the best for her fatherless young son. Her décolleté dress and fashionable coiffure, bedizened with pearls, suggests that she continued to make the best of herself, despite her bereavement. Presumably this pair of medallions was carved in the same campaign of family portraiture as the medallion of James Mackenzie (1696), that of his father and the bust of his uncle, when they were all patronising, perhaps with some excitement, the newly arrived Monsieur Le Marchand. If one knew the date of the sitting, one could calculate the dates of birth of Margaret and her little son George.

10*
George Mackenzie of Rosehaugh (c.1686-1707) 1696-1700
Portrait medallion; profile to the right, with long hair and classical armour
8×6.5 ($3\frac{1}{8} \times 2\frac{9}{16}$)
Private Collection
Condition: very fine
Inscr: (round the upper rim, partly hidden by the frame) GEORGE MACKENZIE OF ROSHAVCH AET X; (on the ground below the truncation) D.L.MARD.F.

PROV: By family descent

LIT: W. Fraser, *The Earls of Cromartie, their kindred, country and correspondence*, Edinburgh, 1876, pp.72-3

8

10

9

The sitter was the son of Margaret Mackenzie of Rosehaugh (Cat.9) and the medallion was evidently carved as a facing pair with hers, replacing the husband, a more normal subject in such a pair, for he was deceased. Le Marchand applied exactly the same formula for a head and shoulders in classical armour as he did to the medallions of the 1st Earl of Cromartie and his son James (Cats 6, 8), though he reduced the thickness of the cloak in view of the boy's smaller size of chest.

Le Marchand was obviously already sympathetic to the innocent, fresh face of childhood. Yet it is amazing to see how far his powers of modelling had advanced by 1700, only four years later, when he signed the medallion of a similarly juvenile subject, Charles Chester Eyre (Cat.75). By then all dryness of execution had disappeared in favour of a silky soft *sfumato* over the cheeks and forehead, as well as in the hair and drapery folds. He had also abandoned the stereotyped image for a nobleman of armoured shoulders and developed his own powers of observation from life and of modelling what he saw most subtly in wax, and then carving and polishing the ivory into an astoundingly accurate facsimile.

11*

James Drummond, 2nd titular Duke of Perth (1673-1720)
1696-1700
Portrait medallion; profile to right wearing full wig and classical armour
Framed 12.3 × 10.8 ($4\frac{7}{8}$ × $4\frac{1}{4}$)
In the collection of the Grimsthorpe and Drummond Castle Trust
Condition: excellent
Inscr: (on the ground below the truncation) D:L.MARCHAND F.

PROV: By family descent

LIT: J. B. Paul (ed.), *The Scots Peerage . . .*, Edinburgh, 1910, VII, pp.53-4

The subject's father, Sir James Drummond, 4th Earl of Perth, who was Lord Chancellor of Scotland, and his uncle, John, the Secretary of State, aided King James II & VII after his accession in 1685 in attempting to re-impose Roman Catholicism on their country, by issuing a Letter of Indulgence permitting freedom of worship. In reward, they were chosen as two of the first eight Knights appointed to the Order of the Thistle that James had revived on 29 May 1687 at Windsor Castle. The date was the anniversary of the accession to the throne in 1660 of King Charles II, the Restoration of the Royal House of Stewart.

After the flight of James, the staunchly Jacobite 4th Earl was imprisoned in Stirling Castle and then went into exile in 1688, being created Duke by the King in 1696. His son, also significantly christened James, was allowed some freedom. Educated at the Scots College in Paris, he attended the exiled King when he embarked at Brest for Ireland in 1689. He was at the siege of Londonderry, the Battle of the Boyne and the retreat at Limerick and the Pass of Athlone, returning to Scotland in 1692. He stayed there for a few years, but then he went to France, where he was created a Knight of the Thistle by James in 1705.

He joined the Earl of Mar in the rising of 1715 and proved to be one of the ablest Jacobite leaders throughout the insurrection. For this he was attainted in 1716, though he had managed to save his estates by passing them to his son in 1715. He never returned to Scotland, but inherited the title of his father after his death in 1716.

There is a portrait of him painted by Sir John Baptist Medina in the Scottish National Portrait Gallery (ill.). It is by comparison with this image that the subject of the present medallion may be determined, for they share the noble, aquiline nose and pointed chin that are so distinctive. The classical armour in which he is shown is nearly identical to that worn by Louis XIV, the Earl of Leven, and the Mackenzies.

12*

Unidentified Lady of the Drummond family, *c.1696* (?) 1696-1700
Portrait medallion; profile to right, her hair piled high and wearing a fashionable gown
Framed 12.3 × 10.8 ($4\frac{7}{8}$ × $4\frac{1}{4}$)
In the collection of the Grimsthorpe and Drummond Castle Trust
Condition: excellent

11

Sir John Baptist Medina, *James Drummond, 2nd titular Duke of Perth*, Scottish National Portrait Gallery, Edinburgh (1531).

PROV: By family descent

LIT: J. B. Paul (ed.), *The Scots Peerage . . .*, Edinburgh, 1910, VII, p.53

The medallion is paired with that depicting James Drummond, 2nd titular Duke of Perth (Cat.11), and their similarity to those showing the Mackenzies around 1696 suggests that they too date from the last four years of the seventeenth century and from Le Marchand's early sojourn in Edinburgh, rather than his later career in London. However, if its subject were Drummond's wife, it would be unusual that she does not face him. Another stumbling block is that he did not marry Jean Gordon (ill.) until 1706, a date for the portraits that seems far too late in Le Marchand's career in stylistic terms. Furthermore, Jean was born only in 1683 and so would have been only about thirteen years old at the probable time of carving (1696), for which the sitter looks too mature.

Alternative hypotheses as to her identity are tentative. Rather than being his wife, she could be James's sister, Lady Mary Drummond (1675-1729), who married in about 1690 William Lord Keith, afterwards 9th Earl Marischal. She would thus have been a married woman of around twenty-one years of age when the carver first set up shop in Edinburgh, and this is consistent with the subject's apparent age and standing. Furthermore, Le Marchand is thought to have carved later on, around 1715-19, a large portrait plaque of the 10th Earl Marischal (Cat.18).

Otherwise, it has been suggested that the subject may be James Drummond's stepmother, Mary Gordon (daughter of the 3rd Marquess of Huntly), who had married the 4th Earl/1st Duke as his third wife, in 1685. Born in 1646, she would have been about fifty when Le Marchand opened his shop.

This seems a trifle old for the traits of the present sitter. In any case the Scottish National Portrait Gallery has no likeness of her for comparison. She was Lady of the Bedchamber to Mary of Modena in 1701, and therefore presumably left Scotland for France before then, although not necessarily in 1696 with her husband.

13*
The Arms of the Duke of Perth 1696-1700

Circular medallion; in the field above, the motto GANG WARLIE
8.7 (3⅜) diameter
In the collection of the Grimsthorpe and Drummond Castle Trust
Condition: excellent
Inscr: (in the exergue) D.L.M.F.

PROV: By family descent

The correct description of the arms is as follows:[1] 'Or, three bars wavy Gules. Above the Shield is placed His Lordship's coronet and thereon a helmet befitting his degree with a Mantle Gules doubled Ermine, and for Crest a ducal crown and thereon a sleuth-hound Proper collared and leashed Gules. Above the Crest the Motto "GANG WARRILY". On a Compartment below the Shield are set for Supporters two savages wreathed about the head and middle with oak leaves Proper each carrying a baton on his shoulder and standing on caltraps.'

This is a modern interpretation of the blazon as it appears in the Public Register of All Arms and Bearings in Scotland c.1672, and at that date all were required to hand in their arms for registration, though frequently without a precise date. This recording, however, must have taken place some time between 1672 and 1689, inasmuch as James Drummond is clearly described as the Earl of Perth. The 3rd Earl died in 1675, well before the possible date of carving of the ivory, and in any case before the revival of the Order of the Thistle by King James II & VII in 1687, the collar of which is shown here. Furthermore, the coronet is that of a Duke.

The 4th Earl of Perth was chosen as one of the first Knights of the Thistle in 1687, and was created Duke of Perth by James by a Patent signed at Dublin on 10 March 1689, but does not seem to have assumed the title until 24 September 1701 when, at the first meeting of the Council of the titular King James VIII (James Francis Edward Stewart), he was declared Duke. The Earl of Manchester, English Ambassador in

12

Anonymous miniaturist, *Jean Drummond, Duchess of Perth*, Collection of the Grimsthorpe and Drummond Castle Trust.

13

Paris, in letters dated 26 and 28 September 1701, confirms this and states that 'Lord Perth is to be a Duke by an old Patent'.

In our present state of knowledge about Le Marchand's career, it seems unlikely that the medallion was carved as late as this, in 1701, for he was by then probably in London, while it is equally unlikely to have been carved before he was permitted to open his shop in Edinburgh on 12 February 1696. Now the exiled 4th Earl was appointed Governor to the Prince of Wales at Saint-Germain (see Cat.15) in that very year, and so perhaps the medallion was carved immediately after this prestigious event, in the very first months of the carver's activity in Edinburgh.

The Lyon Clerk points out – interestingly – that the style of showing the mantle or pavilion behind the shield, coronet and supporters is continental, and may reflect Le Marchand's background in France.

The supporters, in heraldic parlance, 'savages', or wild-men bearing clubs, which were favourites with the Scots, constitute an early, if not the first (see Cat.15), example of David's style of carving figures, and in spite of the limitations imposed by their heraldic context, they are posed most competently in an elegant, Herculean *contrapposto*.

1 I am grateful to Mrs C. G. W. Roads MVO, Lyon Clerk and Keeper of the Records, Court of the Lord Lyon, Edinburgh, for her professional help with the description of the arms, which is quoted verbatim, and for her report on the implications for the date of the medallion

14*
King James II of England and VII of Scotland (1633-1701)
1700-10
Portrait medallion; the King shown laureate and in profile to the left
9.8 × 7.6 ($3\frac{7}{8}$ × 3)
In the collection of the Grimsthorpe and Drummond Castle Trust
Condition: excellent

PROV: By family descent

LIT: R. K. Marshall (ed.), *Dynasty: The Royal House of Stewart*, exh.cat. Scottish National Portrait Gallery/Royal Museum of Scotland (Edinburgh, 1990), pp.81-6

This unpublished image of James is an important discovery, both for the iconography of the King and because it adds another crowned head to the *oeuvre* of Le Marchand. Although it is not signed, it is still today in the company of two other medallions that are, in Drummond Castle (Cats 11, 13), descended as a group within a staunchly Jacobite family. Furthermore, its style is inimitably that of the mature Le Marchand, begging comparison with such portraits as those of Marlborough and of King George I (Cats 21, 32-5). Indeed, it seems to show a knowledge of the very precise, dry medallic image carved by Cavalier of James's successor, King William III around 1690 (ill.p.16).

The portrait is unlikely to have been carved from life, for the King had gone into exile on the continent before David had carved his first ivory. In any case, the depth of cutting and assured handling of the features, combined with the expert placing of the profile to fill the oval field, suggest a date after his initial period in Edinburgh. The carver doubtless remained in touch with some of his Scottish patrons, among them the Jacobite families, and this deliberately laureate image of 'the King across the Water' was probably carved covertly for one of the Drummonds. This may explain why its author was careful to omit his initials from this particular portrait, despite its obvious excellence and the prominence of its regal sitter, which under normal circumstances most artists would have been keen to vaunt. Quite apart from his Protestant British patrons, his fellow Huguenots might well have looked askance at his serving the pro-Catholic, Stewart faction. Those were troubled times indeed.

14

Jan Smeltzing, *The Arrival of King James II of England and VII of Scotland in France*, silver medal, 1689, British Museum, London (CM George III Coll., English Medal AR73).

The King's likeness seems to have been borrowed from that on a silver medal by Jan Smeltzing recording events surrounding James's flight to France and good reception by King Louis XIV in 1689 (ill.p.60).[1] For all this, it is no copy: David raised the head and near shoulder into higher relief from the neutral background, amplified the folds of drapery and enriched Smeltzing's dry, linear patterning of the hair, breathing life into an accurate portrait by a competent die-cutter and transforming it into an entrancing miniature sculpture.

1 Franks and Gruber, 1885/1904/II, I, pp.652, 7, pl.LXIX

15*
Attributed to Le Marchand
An Allegorical Scene probably celebrating the Birth of Prince James Francis Edward Stewart, 'The Old Pretender' (1688-1766)
*c.*1696
Relief, probably the lid of a counter-box
Dimensions unknown
Private Collection (unknown; photograph in the archives of the Scottish National Portrait Gallery, Ph.IV 94-82)

LIT: Dalton, 1909, pp.147-8, pl.CIV, nos 432-40, p.154, no.474; R. K. Marshall (ed.), *Dynasty: The Royal House of Stewart*, exh.cat. Scottish National Portrait Gallery/Royal Museum of Scotland (Edinburgh, 1990), p.98

This unpublished and presumably quite small relief apparently celebrates the birth on 10 June 1688 of a male heir to James II & VII, 'long after everyone had given up hope of Mary Beatrice bearing a living son. On 9 December, his mother disguised herself as a laundress, wrapped the baby up like a bundle of washing and crept out of the palace of Whitehall with his two nurses to escape to France. The exiled Stewarts were given the Palace of Saint Germain by Louis XIV, and there the child was brought up . . . Nine years later James VII suffered a stroke and, as he lay dying, Louis XIV promised to recognize his son as King James VIII & III. In 1713, however, Louis made peace with Britain and, as a result, James was forced to leave France, settling first in Avignon, then in Bologna and finally in Rome.'[1]

In the relief, King James and his Queen are shown as diminutive seated figures, with angels hovering and holding open a cloth of state beneath a baldaquin, as well as proffering crowns over their heads. The royal couple each gesture with one outstretched hand towards a ribbon inscribed with a motto '..EX DIE..', which is an inaccurate rendering of the motto of the Prince of Wales, 'ICH DIEN'. In any case the disproportionately large coronet above has projecting through it the three ostrich feathers that are the insignia of the Prince of Wales. The infant meanwhile, large by comparison with his parents (see below), stands – nude save for a swathe of cloak - in an amusingly adult, classical, heroic pose, with his right wrist resting on his hip and his left hand held out, like a veritable monarch.

The relief may be attributed to Le Marchand on stylistic and circumstantial evidence. The emphasis on the perspective, albeit faulty, of the paved floor recalls his signed relief of the *Miracle of Christ healing the Man with the Withered Hand* (Cat.66), as do the thin ankles, slightly uncertain poses and fluid, waxy-looking patterns of drapery. The emphasis on surrounding incidentals, and the treatment of the ankles, feet and dainty, gesticulating hands and fingers, as well as of the plump cheeks, also recall the much later signed plaque depicting Mathew Raper III (Cat.64). The figures are also consistent with the nearly nude supporters of the coat-of-arms of the Duke of Perth, which is nearer in date (Cat.13).

15

Closest of all are the figures in a larger plaque attributed independently to Le Marchand by Dr Christian Theuerkauff and accepted as such by the present writer: it shows *Apollo and the Muses on Mount Parnassus* (Cat.98). The Morellian idiosyncracies of style in the two reliefs are to all intents and purposes identical. One need only compare the muse seated in the right foreground with Queen Mary Beatrice, or that of Apollo himself with King James.

Now that one knows that Le Marchand was patronised by prominent Jacobites, an attribution to him of this currently missing relief strongly recommends itself. The birth of a Prince of Wales, albeit under unpropitious circumstances, gave greater substance to the claims of the Stewarts to the rightful succession and he and his heir were indeed to prove strong contenders for the throne of Great Britain. The politically sensitive subject may once again have suggested to the carver the wisdom of refraining from applying his signature.

The question of its date then arises. The Stewarts would obviously have wished to celebrate the birth of the heir as soon as was practicable after the arrival of him and his mother in France. If Le Marchand was still living there, as cannot be ruled out (see p.13), and if the portrait relief showing perhaps Vauban is by him and not a relation, thus proving him to have been a competent carver by the age of fifteen, then this composition could have been carved in France from around 1689. Indeed, James II & VII commissioned in Paris in the early 1690s a number of portraits of his son and heir from the famous French portraitist Nicolas de Largillière, who had worked for the royal couple previously in London, emphasising the child's identity by the inclusion of the feathers; medals were also struck as dynastic propaganda. In one dated 1691 (Marshall, *op.cit.*, pl.121), the Prince looks older than his then three years of age, and his pose is reminiscent of an infant Hercules in his cradle, though he is caressing a spaniel – a breed favoured by the Stewarts – and not strangling snakes; this comparison would have occurred to any literate observer at the time and was doubtless deliberate, in order to indicate the child's health and fitness to inherit the throne.

Failing this, it could have been carved retrospectively at the behest of one of David's Jacobite patrons after his establishment in Edinburgh in 1696, and probably before his move to London, *c.*1700. If this were the case, it would serve to explain the appearance and size in proportion to his parents of the Prince of Wales, who, as has been remarked, is shown not as a new-born infant, but as a little boy, possibly as old as seven or eight. The scene would then be a more plausible representation of the actual state of affairs in the mid-1690s.

It may be no coincidence that in 1696 one of Le Marchand's known patrons, the 1st titular Duke of Perth, was appointed Governor to the Prince of Wales, and so would have had a specific and immediate motive for such a commission, as was the case with the Drummond coat-of-arms crowned with the coronet appropriate to a Duke, the rank to which he was elevated in the same year (Cat.13).

Although the owner and whereabouts of the plaque are not recorded, the fact that the photograph is preserved in Edinburgh suggests that they were and possibly still are in Scotland. It is no mystery how or why the piece should have been preserved lovingly there!

Among a series of counter-boxes in the British Museum that are similar in size (*c.*8 cm or $3\frac{1}{4}$ in long) is one whose subject is virtually identical (Dalton, 1909, no.439) and another that is closely related (Dalton, 1909, no.438), both with the motto spelt ICK DIEN. Dalton believed the Stuart Prince of Wales in question to be Charles Edward Stuart ('Bonnie Prince Charlie'), who was born in 1720, and therefore he dated the counter-boxes by the apparent age of the infant to 1724-5. While this cannot be ruled out, and it would still notionally permit Le Marchand to be the author, albeit in old age, it seems more likely that all the boxes depict the 'Old Pretender', and not the 'Young Pretender'.

The heads of the parents are too small for their features to be accurate likenesses: therefore, to distinguish James II from his son, the 'Old Pretender', or their wives, Mary of Modena from Maria Clementina Sobieska, is out of the question. The only extra clue – and it proves to be a vital one – lies in the identity of the *second* infant held in its mother's arms on the variant counter-box (Dalton, 1909, no.438), for the couples differ in the gender of their second offspring. James II had a daughter, Louise Maria Theresa (*b.*1692), whereas the 'Old Pretender' had a second son, Henry Benedict Stewart (*b.*1725) – the last of the line, later known as Cardinal York.

Now the baby held by its mother is totally naked and its private parts are not visible, owing to the position of the legs. While this appears to leave the matter open, the facts that the infant is protectively held by its mother and its sex is *not* emphasised, suggest that it is a girl, by contrast with the Prince of Wales who is distinguished as a male heir by being next to his father and having one hand on the back of Father Time. If this line of argument is followed, then the scene can only depict James II and his children, the second of which was indeed female.

Furthermore, this relief has certain features in common with the missing one, such as the rendering of the ground as a surface striated with lines in an approximation of perspective, that are not found on the other box with the identical scene in the British Museum. Therefore, there may have been more than one hand involved in any case.

That such boxes were being produced as early as around 1700 is indicated by four other ones in the British Museum with the royal arms carved on their lids (Dalton, 1909, nos 432-6), for they are 'Stated to have been given by Sarah, Duchess of Marlborough to Queen Anne as a New Year gift'. If this is true, it corroborates the case stated above for an earlier dating of those showing a Stewart Prince of Wales and adds circumstantial evidence to the ascription of at least the missing one to Le Marchand, for he was definitely in touch with the Marlboroughs.

Furthermore, another box, this time oval (Dalton, 1909, no.437), appears to show Queen Anne in a sea-chariot; while another rectangular one (Dalton, 1909, no.474) shows mythological figures around the arms of Philippe, Duke of Orleans (1674-1723). Both these royal subjects are appropriate to the span of Le Marchand's career. On the last related box in the British Museum, one showing the *Murder of Cain by Abel* (Dalton, 1909, no.440), the minute, but muscular, nude male figures in strife certainly bear comparison with the club-bearing supporters of the coat-of-arms of the Duke of Perth (Cat.13).

Nevertheless, the absence of his initials from any of these counter-boxes leaves all these potential ascriptions hypothetical, and it might still be argued that the stylistic association may be generically with French ivory carving of the period, rather than with Le Marchand in particular.

1. Marshall, *op.cit.*, p.98

16
Unidentified Nobleman in Armour 1696-1700
Portrait medallion; profile to the right, wearing classical armour
18.5 × 7.5 (3⅜ × 2¾)
Collection of Lord Thomson of Fleet, Toronto
Condition: good
Inscr: (on the ground below the truncation) D.L.M.

PROV: Sotheby's, 9 April 1973, lot 151

In spite of a degree of idealisation, the pronounced bridge of the nose is evident, as well as the sharply projecting tip of the chin, and the face may be presumed to be narrow and delicate, rather than fleshy.

The use of Le Marchand's favourite formula for the classically armoured shoulders, the treatment of the hair – perhaps the subject's own, and not a wig – and the minute capitals used in the signature all point to this medallion being from the carver's sojourn in Edinburgh, or shortly thereafter, and so the subject may be a Scot.

The only difference is the integrally carved moulded rim that the other Scottish medallions do not have, as they were evidently meant to be framed. It would help to protect the image from rubbing such as might occur if it were carried about the person, and indeed no such wear has occurred.

17
After Le Marchand
Anonymous Nobleman 1696-1700
Portrait medallion; profile to the right
8 × 5.9 (3⅛ × 2⁵⁄₁₆)
The National Museum, Stockholm (1067.1922)
Condition: good

This medallion may be meant to depict the same sitter as an initialled one (Cat.16), even down to details of the curls in the wig, though the

shape of the nose is less pronounced. The foreshortening of the shoulders is, however, less convincingly treated, and the drapery is more schematically rendered. The bust also appears physically to project less, and the conclusion to be drawn is that it is a copy, albeit probably an early one. It may be the work of one of Le Marchand's apprentices in Edinburgh.

18*
George Keith, 10th Earl Marischal (1693?-1778) 1715-19
Portrait medallion; full face
19.5 × 14 (7⅝ × 5½)
The British Museum, London, MLA 1960, 4-1, 1
Condition: incipient crack in ground at left

PROV: Mrs Collier, Font Hill, Lansdown, Bath (c.1935)

LIT: J. Kerslake, *National Portrait Gallery, Early Georgian Portraits*, London, 1977, I, pp.182-3, no.552, pl.526

The portrait, which is unsigned, has been associated with paintings in the Scottish National Portrait Gallery, the National Portrait Gallery in London, and elsewhere depicting the Jacobite last Earl Marischal, who commanded cavalry at Sheriffmuir in 1715 and led the Spanish Jacobite expedition of 1719. He retired after Glenshiel to the continent, becoming an intimate of Frederick the Great of Prussia, whose ambassador to Paris he became in 1751. He was pardoned by George II in 1759 and succeeded to the Kintore estates in 1761, but was recalled to Prussia by Frederick the Great in 1764.

The unusual image in full face and on a thin plaque of ivory, combined with the treatment of the wig as a series of sinuous, calligraphic curls and rolls, make this portrait conform with the plaques by Le Marchand showing Guy and Newton (Cats 42, 44). The piercing gaze, conveyed by the deeply drilled pupils of the eyes, surrounded by incised irises, is also to be paralleled in most of his busts, *eg* Newton,

16

17

18

Somers and Sambrooke (Cats 47, 37, 58). An attribution to Le Marchand is therefore valid, particularly in view of his earlier connections with Scottish patrons, including some other Jacobites.

Nevertheless, in view of the proposed subject's date of birth and apparent maturity, it cannot date from Le Marchand's initial period in Edinburgh, and probably falls within the span of 1715-19, as indicated by the Earl's fortunes around the time of the Jacobite expeditions of 1715 and before his estates suffered attainder in 1719.

19
Anonymous Gentleman in a Banyan Probably before 1699
Portrait medallion; profile to the right
$8 \times 7 \left(3\frac{1}{8} \times 2\frac{3}{4}\right)$
The National Museum, Stockholm (1079-1922)
Condition: excellent
Inscr: (on the ground below the truncation) D. LE MAR.D.F.

LIT: Julius, 1926, pp.86-7, pl.22; M. H. Swain, 'The Nightgown of Governor Jonathan Trumbull', *Wadsworth Atheneum*, Sixth Series, vol. VI, no.3, Winter 1970, pp.28-33; M. H. Swain, 'Men's Nightgowns of the Eighteenth Century', *Waffen und Kostümkunde*, 1972, pp.41-8

It was fashionable in the 1670s to 1690s to wear silk imported from Persia, especially when made up for gentlemen in the form of a loose house-coat called a 'banyan', sometimes with a matching turban. A characteristic example is worn in the self-portrait by Antonio Verrio in the National Portrait Gallery (no.2980); while accurate miniature ones are part of the apparel of the celebrated dolls Lord and Lady Clapham in the Victoria & Albert Museum.

However, in 1699 an Act of Parliament forbade the use and wear of Eastern silks, and so the likelihood is that this portrait was produced before then. Such a dating is corroborated stylistically by the relatively simple carving of the wig and the epigraphy of the signature and the low relief of the whole which accord with Le Marchand's portraits of Scottish sitters from 1696 and soon thereafter.

19

London and the Court

Le Marchand had probably moved to London by 1700, perhaps following the death of his predecessor in portraiture in ivory, Jean Cavalier (see ills pp.16, 74), for several of his major portraits of metropolitan subjects are dated between then and 1705. He was documented in the capital by 1705, was naturalised in 1709, and, after an artistically fruitful career, died a pauper in the French Hospital in 1726.

Among the patrons who flocked to him were royalty – Queen Anne and King George I – and nobility – The Duke of Marlborough and his pretty daughter Anne, Countess of Sunderland, as well as the Earl of Peterborough and the Privy Councillor, Thomas Brodrick PC.

20★ (Plate 13)
Queen Anne (1665-1714) 1702-12
Portrait medallion; profile to the left
12.75 (5)
Collection of Lord Thomson of Fleet, Toronto
Condition: good
Inscr: (on the ground below the truncation of the shoulder) D.L.M.

PROV: Sotheby's, 2 July 1973, lot 112

LIT: National Portrait Gallery, *Royal Faces: 900 Years of British Monarchy*, London, 1977, p.38, repr.

The source for this image is the profile portrait of Anne by Kneller (1702), which was engraved by J. Simon (See P. A. S. Phillips, *John Obrisset*, London, 1931, p.63). Obrisset produced similar portraits on his pressed horn snuff-boxes in 1705, as did John Croker on his medal of 1707, which was struck to commemorate the Union of England and Scotland (Franks and Gruber, 1885/1904/11).

A historian specialising in the period, Miss Margaret Toynbee, of Oxford, wrote of the medallion in a letter of 1977, 'although there are general similarities with the Kneller profile versions and the medals stated to be derived from them, the Le Marchand strikes one as a vigorous independent approach. Could it possibly have been executed *ad vivum*?'

However, David normally stated explicitly after his signature when he had worked from life (see *eg* Cats 31, 44), and so this seems unlikely, in spite of the almost 'speaking' likeness.

21★
John Churchill, 1st Duke of Marlborough (1650-1722) 1700-10
Portrait medallion; profile to the right
$13 \times 10.8 \left(5\frac{1}{8} \times 4\frac{1}{2}\right)$
The Victoria & Albert Museum, London, A.5-1950
Condition: good
Inscr: (on the ground below the truncation of the shoulder) D.L.M.F.

PROV: Henry Oppenheimer; E. L. Paget (sale Sotheby's, 11 October 1949, lot 84, pl.XII); bought by A. Spero (£32); Given to the Victoria & Albert Museum by Dr W. L. Hildburgh FSA

EXH: BFAC, 1923, no.221, pl.LII; Museum of London, 1985, p.210, cat.no.307

LIT: Longhurst, 1926, pp.59, 114, no.LXXVII, pl.54; Avery, 1984, p.113

David Le Marchand also executed portrait busts of Marlborough's daughter, Anne Churchill, Countess of Sunderland, one of which is in the same collection (see Cat.25), whilst two others are also known (see Cats 24,26). John Churchill, born in Devon and educated at St Paul's, made progress at the Court of Charles II as the follower of James, Duke of York, whose daughter Anne formed a close friendship with his beautiful and distinguished wife Sarah Churchill. He fought under the Duke of York at sea (1672), under Turenne (1673) and at Sedgemoor (1685); he became Baron in 1682. His desertion in 1688 helped to induce James II's flight, and though rewarded with an earldom, he appears to have considered abandoning William III in 1692, for which he was for a time in disgrace.

However, on the accession of Anne (1702) he became Commander-in-Chief of the allied forces in the War of the Spanish Succession. By his remarkable march to Blenheim (1704) and by his victory there he wrested the initiative from the French, subsequently pressing them hard in the Netherlands, defeating them at Ramillies (1706), Oudenarde (1708), Malplaquet (1709) and breaking their vaunted Ne Plus Ultra line without a battle (1711). But both his ascendancy and the protracted war had become irksome to the Queen and the country, and, supported by a Tory majority, she dismissed him in 1711.

He then prepared to support the Hanoverian Succession, if necessary by force: when this occurred peacefully in 1714, he resumed his position of Commander-in-Chief. His greatest triumph was to restore mobility to battle, but his diplomacy, which kept the Grand Alliance together, was almost as distinguished.

The Duke of Marlborough also had a definite interest in sculpture, for in 1710, with the advice of Vanbrugh, architect of Blenheim Palace, he ordered from Soldani in Florence four life-size bronze statues after famous antiquities in the Tribuna of the Uffizi Gallery, by kind permission of Grand Duke Cosimo III.[1]

1 A. Ciechanowiecki and G. Seagrim, 'Soldani's Blenheim Commission and other Bronze Sculptures after the Antique', in *Festschrift Klaus Lankheit*, Cologne, 1973, pp.180-4, pls 85-93

22*

After a model attributed to Le Marchand
Anonymous Lady, possibly Sarah, Duchess of Marlborough
*c.*1770
Wax portrait medallion; profile to the left
$11.7 \times 9.5 \times 2.2$ $(4\frac{5}{8} \times 3\frac{3}{4} \times \frac{7}{8})$
Wedgwood Museum, Barlaston (No.2419)
Condition: loss to far right segment of ground

PROV: Old factory site

The medallion is deeply modelled, with the drapery tucked under the truncation of the shoulder. There is no trace of a signature. The sitter's hair is casually coiffed in a chignon with pearls and a ribbon, one end flying out loose on the ground behind her head. These features relate the portrait closely to that of Queen Anne (Cat.20), while showing a slightly slimmer woman, with a more pointed nose.

The near-duplication of the Queen's image might have caused offence had the sitter not been someone in her intimate circle, and so her confidante, Sarah, Duchess of Marlborough, would be a strong candidate, though so far no profile of her has been discovered with which to compare the ivory. There is good reason to suppose that Le Marchand might have portrayed Sarah, for he portrayed John Churchill, her famous husband (Cat.21), as well as their pretty daughter Anne, later Countess of Sunderland (Cats 24-6). Sarah was not one to be left out, and if this medallion does show her, she would be appropriately facing that of her husband, who is shown in profile to the right. They are of similar size, around 13 cm (5 in) high, with his one being slightly the larger.

21

23

22

23*
After a model attributed to Le Marchand
Anonymous Lady *c.*1770
Wax portrait medallion; profile to the right
12.7 × 10 (5 × 3$\frac{15}{16}$)
Wedgwood Museum, Barlaston (No.2385)

PROV: Old factory site

This medallion is attributed to Le Marchand on the grounds of its association in the Wedgwood stock-in-trade with, and general similarity to, the one (Cat.22) that is modelled on his signed ivory of Queen Anne (Cat.20). The treatment of the hair is particularly close, with the fluent, sinuous loose curls, but the handling of the sleeve of her robe is not quite so typical of Le Marchand's usual technique. One has to bear in mind the presence in London alongside David of a fellow countryman and co-religionist, who is known to have modelled portraits in wax and to have carved them in ivory too, Mathieu Gosset (see p.18).

24*
Anne Churchill, Countess of Sunderland (1683-1716) *c.*1699
Bust
11 (4$\frac{1}{4}$)
The Earl Spencer, Althorp
Condition: slight cracking
Inscr: (on the back) D.L.M.

PROV: Purchased by the late Lord Spencer (1923) from the Warren Galleries

LIT: H. Walpole, *Reminiscences: written in 1788, for the amusement of Miss Mary and Miss Agnes B***y*, London, 1819, p.69; Maclagan and Longhurst, 1929, II, p.84; D. Green, *Queen Anne*, London, 1970

Other examples: see Cats 25, 26

Anne Churchill, the second daughter of John Churchill, 1st Duke of Marlborough was a Beauty, and married in 1699 Charles Spencer, 3rd Earl of Sunderland. Le Marchand's three portrait busts may date from around the time of her wedding, or just after 1700, when she was sixteen, or, like Kneller's painting of her in the National Portrait Gallery (no.803), from *c.*1710. They were perhaps made for different members of the families. Anne was god-daughter of Queen Anne and was given £5000 by the monarch on her wedding. She and her elder sister Harriet were both Ladies of the Bedchamber and sometimes substituted for their mother, Sarah, Duchess of Marlborough, as Mistress of Queen Anne's Wardrobe (Green, *op.cit.*, p.137). Even so, Anne, toast of the Kit Kat Club as 'the little Whig', was disliked after her marriage by the Queen on account of her husband (Green, *op.cit.*, p.184).

Horace Walpole, writing his *Reminiscences* in 1788, recalled Anne as the most beautiful of Sarah's 'four charming daughters', and that she 'was a great politician; and having, like her mother, a most beautiful head of hair, used, while combing it at her toilet, to receive men whose votes or interest she wished to influence'.

24

25

26

25*

Anne Churchill, Countess of Sunderland (1683-1716) *c.*1699
Bust
13 (5)
The Victoria & Albert Museum, London, A.67-1926
Condition: good
Inscr: (on the back) D.L.M.

PROV: Bequeathed by Lt-Col G. B. Croft-Lyons FSA

EXH: BFAC, 1923, no.219, pl.LII

LIT: Longhurst, 1926, no.LXXVI, pp.59, 113, pl.53; Victoria & Albert Museum *Review*, 1926, p.5; Maclagan and Longhurst, 1926, II, p.84, pl.LXXII

Other, variant, examples: see Cats 24, 26

Anne is shown in a loose chemise, such as she might have worn at the Whiggish political levées recorded by Horace Walpole (see Cat.24).

This imagery of casual femininity and youthful charm may have been known to Michael Rysbrack, for his marble bust of 1723 showing Lady Margaret Cavendish-Holles-Harley at Welbeck Woodhouse, Nottinghamshire, is similarly arranged.[1] If so, he was following a precedent set by Le Marchand perhaps as long as a quarter of a century earlier.

1 M. I. Webb, *Michael Rysbrack Sculptor*, London, 1954, p.217, fig.35

26

Anne Churchill, Countess of Sunderland (1683-1716) *c.*1699
Bust
14 ($5\frac{1}{2}$)
The Metropolitan Museum of Art, New York; Untermyer Collection, 1974.28.148
Condition: cracking; ivory carved in two pieces; neck fitted into bodice; jewel missing from clasp; mounted on later ebony socle
Inscr: (on the reverse) L.M.F.

PROV: With Cyril Humphris, London; Judge Irwin Untermyer, New York (purchased June 1966); Bequeathed to the Metropolitan Museum of Art, New York

LIT: J. Draper, *The Untermyer Collection*, Metropolitan Museum of Art, New York, 1977, no.331

Other examples: see Cats 24, 25

The brevity of the initials of the signature, omitting the normal 'D', is slightly disquieting. This bust is unique in Le Marchand's *oeuvre* in being pieced together from two separately carved components, the head and the shoulders. This accounts for the unusual geometric line that is only partially disguised by serving as the edge of the hem of the neckline of the dress. The attached jewel, also a unique interpolation, was perhaps also designed to distract the eye from this shortcoming, perhaps imposed by accidental damage to one or other part in the carving process, rendering a replacement necessary.

27

Style of Le Marchand
Louisa, Countess of Berkeley (*d.*1717) 1711
Portrait medallion; profile to the left
6.4 × 5 ($2\frac{1}{2}$ × 2)
Formerly David Daniels Collection, New York
Condition: good
Inscr: (in relief lettering within sunken areas) LOUISA COMITISSA DE BERKLEY [*sic*] AO 1711.

PROV: James Coats, London, 1967

LIT: C. Avery, in Minneapolis Institute of Arts, *Sculpture from the David Daniels Collection*, exh.cat., Minneapolis, 1979, p.74, no.27

The Countess is shown in left profile, her dress loosely buttoned on her shoulder. Her hair is knotted at the back of her head and a long curly strand falls over her right shoulder.

Louisa was the elder daughter of the 1st Duke of Richmond and Lennox, who was an illegitimate son of King Charles II by Louise Renée de Penancoet de Kéroualle, Duchess of Portsmouth (*d.*1734). She married James, 3rd Earl of Berkeley KG, a distinguished naval officer, who had summons to Parliament in 1704 as Lord de Berkeley. He was made Lord Lieutenant of the county of Gloucester in 1710 and of the county of Lincoln in 1727. He was also Vice-Admiral of Great Britain.

The Countess is shown in fashionable *déshabillé* and it is probable that this ivory portrait was carved as a keep-sake for her husband. The medallion is smaller than most of those by Le Marchand and is not signed. Furthermore, the technique of counter-sinking the inscription is not one employed by him elsewhere. Nonetheless, the treatment of the Countess's swan-like neck and loosely waving hair is similar to David's style as manifested in his busts of the Countess of Sunderland (Cats 24-6).

27

28 (Plate 5)

Noblewoman sitting with her daughter and a pet whippet

(perhaps Anne, Countess of Sunderland, with her daughter Anne, later Viscountess Bateman) *c*.1710

Plaque; the mother seated at the right, with her daughter at the left standing behind her while both play with the prancing pet and engage the beholder with a direct, full-face stare

19 × 13 × 3.2 ($7\frac{1}{2}$ × $5\frac{1}{8}$ × $1\frac{1}{4}$)

Private Collection

Condition: excellent, save for a break in the mother's left thumb, which may be a replacement. Minute toolmarks are visible over both faces, so that the flesh is matt, rather than highly polished, and thus appears more soft and lifelike. The reverse is plain

Inscr: (at lower left) DLM

Small printed paper label glued to the reverse of the frame, filled in with sepia ink: Midland Counties Art Museum

PROV: Collection of the Dukes of Newcastle, Clumber, by 1879

EXH: Lent to Nottingham Castle, The Midland Counties Art Museum, 1879-84/5.[1]

This magnificent relief plaque with a double portrait unique in Le Marchand's *oeuvre* is unpublished. It rivals in attractiveness the portrait of Mathew Raper III in the family library (Cat.64) and the full-face image of Newton in a wig (Cat.44).

The identities of the extremely beautiful, youngish and vivacious mother and her pretty ten-year-old daughter are not inscribed or otherwise indicated on the plaque of ivory, but the paper label glued to the backing of the frame provides some clues.

After a disastrous fire at Clumber, Nottinghamshire, the house of the Dukes of Newcastle, the plaque was among many works of art that were lent temporarily, for safe-keeping and display to the public, to the new museum in Nottingham Castle, between 1879 and 1884/5, but then returned. It does not feature in the catalogue of the sale of the remaining contents of Clumber held at the house in 1937,[2] and may have been disposed of separately, either earlier or later.

From this evidence it appears that the ladies depicted are likely to be related to the Dukes of Newcastle. The relevant Duke is Thomas Pelham-Holles, Duke of Newcastle upon Tyne, and of Newcastle-under-Lyme, statesman (1693-1768). On the death of Queen Anne he declared for the House of Brunswick. He raised a troop for service against the Pretender and was rewarded with the title of Marquis of Clare and Duke of Newcastle upon Tyne (11 August 1715). By the second marriage of his brother-in-law Charles, 2nd Viscount Townshend, with Dorothy Walpole, sister of Sir Robert Walpole, he was brought into intimate relations with the latter, and this formed the background to his further career.

The Duke's marriage on 2 April 1717 to Lady Henrietta, eldest daughter of Francis, 2nd Earl of Godolphin (and grand-daughter of John Churchill, Duke of Marlborough), connected him with Charles Spencer, 3rd Earl of Sunderland. If the lady here represented is Henrietta, and the girl her daughter, in view of the latter's apparent age of eight-to-ten-years-old, the portrait could only date from the very end of Le Marchand's activity, *c*.1725. This seems unlikely, and therefore one may have to look to immediate forebears instead.

The connection with the Churchills and Sunderlands (mentioned in the *Dictionary of National Biography*) puts one in mind of Le Marchand's portrait medallion of John, the putative one of Sarah, and the busts of their daughter Anne. Both the present ladies closely resemble the bust of Anne, Countess of Sunderland, in the Victoria & Albert Museum (Cat.25), and it seems possible that here she is the mother, with little Anne, her daughter. The ivory would thus probably date from before Anne (senior's) death in 1716, and a date *c*.1710 is indicated by the fact that Anne (junior) married in 1720 William, 1st Viscount Bateman.

An explanation of how the ivory plaque might have come into the possession of the Dukes of Newcastle is to be found in the fact that the first wife of Charles Sunderland had been Arabella, daughter and co-heir of the 2nd Duke of Newcastle, who died on 2 June 1698.[3]

Whether the whippet has a particular significance beyond that of a pet, perhaps an heraldic one, remains to be established.

The plaque demonstrates the carver's uncanny ability to make his sitters seem to be alive and to wish to communicate directly with not only their near and dear, or contemporary admirers, but also with posterity, an ability which sets him in the forefront of portraitists in ivory from all over Europe, a forerunner and rival of the great school of British portrait sculpture of the first half of the eighteenth century, and the equivalent of painters such as Kneller and Highmore, to name but the best known.

1   *2nd Annual Report of the Castle Museum Committee, to 31 October 1879*, p.10: 'In consequence of the fire at Clumber House, the Trustees of the Duke of Newcastle very gladly accepted the offer of the Committee to take charge of any works of art they thought desirable . . . All the Pictures, porcelain, sculpture, furniture, etc. that were not damaged by the fire were selected . . . The sculpture consists of busts and groups; . . . The whole of the objects are in cases in one room and each is labelled'
    6th Report of the Science and Art Museum Committee, Nottingham Castle; including the Annual Report of the Castle Museum Committee to 12 March 1885, p.20: 'The Director's and Curator's Report . . . The large and splendid collection lent by the Trustees of the Duke of Newcastle, a portion of which was lent at the opening of the Museum, has been returned to Clumber . . . everything was returned without accident'

2   Christie's, 19-22 October 1937, *Catalogue of the Remaining Contents of the Mansion of Clumber. The Property of The Honourable the Earl of Lincoln, Inherited under the Will of the late Henry Pelham Archibald Douglas Pelham-Clinton, Seventh Duke of Newcastle*

3   I am grateful to Anthony Du Boulay FSA, for his research into the respective pedigrees and communicating these results

29* (Plate 16)

Anonymous Nobleman (possibly Louis, Dauphin of France, *d*.1711)

1700

Bust

15 (6)

The National Trust, Anglesey Abbey, Cambridgeshire

Condition: slight cracking – but generally good

Inscr: (on the reverse) D.D / LE / MARCHAND / SCULT. / AN.DO. 1700

PROV: Unknown French collection (19th century, judging from the paper label); Sotheby's, 22 February 1949, lot 66 (unsold); Lord Fairhaven

LIT: Houfe, 1971, p.66, fig.1

There is a paper label on the bottom of the wooden pedestal with the remains of an inscription in ink which may indicate that the sitter is the Grand Dauphin ('Monseigneur'): 'Mourut de la petite Vérole 14me d'Avril 17[1]1 age de . . . fut inhumé a St De[nis]'. Accordingly, this bust has traditionally been described as Louis the Grand Dauphin (1661-1711), son of King Louis XIV, but it does not particularly resemble the bronze bust of *c*.1700 by Girardon.

As this is Le Marchand's earliest portrait bust on a grand scale (within the constraints imposed by the dimensions of a tusk of ivory), it is disappointing that the identity of the subject is, if one discounts the traditional suggestion, unknown. The pseudo-Roman armour is found on some of Le Marchand's portraits of Scottish noblemen, and, given the early date of 1700, it may even represent one of them, rather than a Frenchman, or a patron in London.

30*

Charles Mordaunt, 3rd Earl of Peterborough and 1st Earl of Monmouth of the second creation (1658-1735) 1704-13
Portrait medallion; head full frontal, armoured chest set at an oblique angle to left
21.7 × 16.5 (8½ × 6½)
Collection of Lord Thomson of Fleet, Toronto
Condition: good
Inscr: (on the ground below the truncation) D.L.M. Sc.

PROV: The Rt Hon. Lord Chesham (his sale, Sotheby's, 10 December, 1946, lot 74); Alfred Spero, London (1953)

LIT: *The Concise Dictionary of National Biography*, Oxford, 1882, I, p.899

The identification of the sitter given in the Sotheby's catalogue entry is cautious, though specific, and is sufficiently obscure for it to be taken seriously, as being perhaps the verbal tradition handed down to the then vendor, rather than being dismissed.

Charles Mordaunt was an admiral, general and diplomatist, heavily involved in the complex history of his times. A member of the parliamentary opposition 1680-6, he went to Holland and intrigued against James II & VII, being rewarded by being made a Privy Councillor on the accession of William III in 1689, a Lord of the Bedchamber, First Lord of the Treasury and created Earl of Monmouth. He succeeded his uncle as 3rd Earl of Peterborough in 1697.

Mordaunt advocated the impeachment of Lord Somers (Cat.37), but then in 1702 helped him to translate the *Olynthiacs* and *Philippics* of Demosthenes. He was appointed joint commander with Sir Clowdesley Shovel of the expeditionary force to Spain (1705), with its controversial outcome, resulting in a public inquiry, which he survived (1708). He was chosen as a Knight of the Garter in 1713 and made ambassador extraordinary to the Italian princes, but was recalled on the accession of George I (1714).

He was said to have married the singer Anastasia Robinson (1722) and he corresponded and addressed verses to Mrs Howard. He was a patron of letters and science, numbering among his friends Swift, Pope, Arbuthnot and Gay.

One would guess the age of the portly subject at about forty, and so if the identification is correct, it should have been carved in the first quinquennium of the new century. This would make it around the same time as Le Marchand's bust of Lord Somers (1704), when the two scholars were working on translations of the classics (1702), and so his mind might have been directed towards his interest in the arts, rather than to politics and warfare.

The second quinquennium seems a less likely period, for his career was in turmoil, while after that he would have been too old for the present depiction: furthermore, the St George pendant of the Order of the Garter would hardly have been omitted from an official type of portrait in uniform such as this, and so it would have to antedate 1713.

29

30

31*

King George I (1660-1727), from life *c.*1714
Bust
25 (9¾)
The Victoria & Albert Museum, London, A.12-1931
Condition: ivory darkened and cracked
Inscr: (on back of stand) Le Marchand ad Viv Scul.

PROV: Basildon Park, Pangbourne, Berks (sold Waring & Gillow, 26 October 1920, lot 1075, ill.23B); Bought from Alfred Spero (£175)

Other examples: profile reliefs, see Cats 32-5

Sir Eric Maclagan wrote in support of the acquisition (1931): 'This is almost, if not quite, the largest ivory portrait bust with which I am acquainted, and it is carved with a great deal of power although the model is not an attractive one'.

The occasion when this impressive bust was carved is not known and while it is tempting to suppose that it might have been commissioned shortly after the King's accession in 1714 and arrival in Britain, it appears to show him as older than in the two signed plaques depicting George in contemporary armour (Cats 34-5). This effect may however be exaggerated by the accidental craquelure and darkening of the ivory itself.

The ends of the wig are bagged behind the shoulders, as was customary when on active service.

32*

King George I (1660-1727) 1714-20
Portrait medallion; profile to the right
12 (4¾)
The British Museum, London, No.456
Condition: good
Inscr: (on the truncation of the shoulder) Le Marchand; (and on the ground below the truncation of the shoulder) ad Viv. Scul.

PROV: Given by Sir A.W. Franks KCB, 1895

LIT: Dalton, 1909, no.456, p.152

Other examples: see Cats 31, 33, 34

If this, the bust of the King and the other medallions were not royal commissions, they may have originated with patrons who wished to demonstrate their loyalty to their new Hanoverian king, perhaps to make a political point and/or in gratitude for a favour. One such would be David's avid patron and seemingly close friend, Moses Raper (Cat.65), who was appointed a Gentleman of the Privy Chamber to King George.[1]

1 *Gentleman's Magazine*, 1719. My thanks to Peter Edden for this observation (see Cat.42, note 1)

33*

King George I (1660-1727) 1714-20
Rectangular portrait plaque; profile laureate to right
11 × 8.3 (4⅝ × 3¼)
Private Collection
Condition: triangular repair lower left corner; small loss to upper right corner

PROV: With Mallett at Bourdon House, London[1]

32

LIT: J. P. Smith, *James Tassie 1735-99, modeller in glass, a classical approach*, London, 1995, p.23

The existence of this laureate image of the King had been inferred from an oval medallic relief cast in beeswax (from the Mary Bate Collection and now in the Victoria & Albert Museum), which is very similar to Le Marchand's other portraits of George I.[2]

The pattern of alternating lozenges and round bosses on the epaulettes of the Roman-style cuirass is identical with that used on Le Marchand's signed portrait of the King *all'antica* in the British Museum that was done from life (Cat.32). The treatment of the wig and of the sagging skin under the monarch's chin, not to mention that of the rest of his blunt features, is closely similar too. The bust portion is slightly less deep here, such that the ornamentally curled strapwork ends of the epaulettes are omitted, as are the lower folds of the cloak across the monarch's chest.

Despite the lack of signature, the plaque may therefore confidently be attributed to Le Marchand. This thus constitutes the third slightly diverse image of the King that the carver executed in relief.

1 I am grateful to Mr John Smith for bringing its whereabouts to my attention and to Mr Thomas Woodham-Smith of Mallett at Bourdon House for allowing me to examine it and for agreeing to lend it to the exhibition

2 A.38-1971; bought from Philip Bate for £100. The bust is smaller than on the ivory plaque, suggesting that it was cast from it, or from the original model by Le Marchand. In view of the diverse shapes of background plaque, internal measurements were taken for comparison: [a] vertical, from tip of laurel leaf above, to edge of truncation below: ivory, 10 cm; wax, 9.5 cm; [b] tip of ribbon end behind neck to tip of nose: ivory, 6.5 cm; wax, 5.2 cm. My thanks to Wendy Fisher and Lucy Cullen, colleagues in the Sculpture Collection of the Museum, who kindly facilitated my examination of the wax version

34
King George I (1660-1727) 1714-20
Portrait medallion; profile to the right
16.4 × 14 (6½ × 5½)
Herzog Anton Ulrich-Museum, Braunschweig [Elf.351 (393)]
Condition: perfect
Inscr: (on the truncation of the shoulder) Le Marchad [*sic*]

LIT: Scherer, *c*.1905, pp.25-6, fig.19; Scherer, 1931, p.110, no.351, pl.54

Other examples: see Cats 31-3, 35

This portrait must date from between the accession of George I in 1714 and the death of Le Marchand in 1726. Its presence in the Ducal collection at Braunschweig is explicable through their connection with the House of Hanover.

35[★]
King George I (1660-1727) 1714-20
Portrait medallion; profile to the right
10.2 (4)
Collection of Lord Thomson of Fleet, Toronto
Condition: good
Inscr: (on the truncation of the shoulder) D.L.M.

PROV: Purchased from Montague Marcussen, 1953

Other examples: see Cats 31, 32, 34

This portrait is closely related to the 'Hanoverian' one in Braunschweig, differing only in the pattern of plates of armour on the shoulder, and in the introduction of a fluttering ribbon tying the long locks of hair behind the neck. The initials are neatly disposed and firmly incised with serifs.

33

34

35

36*

The Rt Hon. Thomas Brodrick PC (1654-1730) *c.*1714-20

Portrait medallion; profile to the right

10 × 7.5 (4 × 3)

The British Museum, London, No.460

Condition: good

Inscr: (on the ground below the truncation of the shoulder) D.L.M.

PROV: A.W. Franks; presented to the British Museum, 1882

LIT: Dalton, 1909, no.460, p.152, pl.CIII; Longhurst, 1926, p.60; Houfe, 1971, pp.66-70; Avery, 1984, p.115; Museum of London, 1985, p.208, no.305

A profile bust to the right of Thomas Brodrick, the eldest son of Sir St John Brodrick of Midleton, County Cork. Thomas Brodrick represented his home county in Parliament, 1703, and was later MP for Stockbridge, 1713, and Guildford, 1722. He was joint Comptroller of the Army Accounts, 1708, and appointed a member of the Privy Council to George I, 1714.

According to Vertue, Brodrick, an enthusiastic virtuoso, instigated on 14 February 1721 a change in the Law regarding tax dues levied on imported works of art, whereby they would depend thenceforth on the size of a painting, rather than on its original price.[1]

1 I. Pears, *The Discovery of Painting*, New Haven/London, 1988, p.54, notes 19-20

36

Whig Noblemen and Intellectuals

Within the circle of Le Marchand's patrons certain patterns may be discovered. For example quite early on, in 1706, he carved a splendid bust of Lord Somers, which was later in the possession of Lord Halifax. Both were leading Whigs. The latter, as Charles Montagu, had been an MP since the Revolution of 1689, and as a Lord of the Treasury from 1692 he espoused the concept of the National Debt and the foundation of the Bank of England. This was a stronghold of Huguenot businessmen and investors, and seems to have been the epicentre of Le Marchand's activity, given that his favourite patrons, the Rapers, were Directors, while two of the previously anonymous subjects may have been prominent too in its early years (see below, pp.86-95).

Several of David's sitters by the time that he carved them were famous men of yesteryear. Pepys, for instance, died in 1703 and Locke in 1704, so that it is not clear whether their portraits were from life, or worked up posthumously from other images. Indeed the ivory carver seems to have worked closely with the painter Kneller, and they may even have held joint sittings. Others of his subjects were alive for most, if not all, of his career, and – when they do not bear a date – it is hard to situate them within his *oeuvre* on the grounds of style alone: Wren (*d.*1723), Guy (*d.*1724), Newton (*d.*1727).

Even though two busts in the round of the latter are dated 1714 and 1718, it is difficult to place the reliefs (let alone the secondary busts) chronologically around them with any degree of certainty, or even to know which of these images was the one owned by Sir Isaac himself, for contemporary descriptions tend not to give sufficient data.

The last of David's 'intellectual' subjects was the Reverend William Stukeley, pioneer, though amateur, archaeologist, who was in close touch with the elderly Isaac Newton. Stukeley was the only one to record in his diary an actual sitting for his portrait (1722), as well as regretting the carver's death in 1726.

37*

John Somers, Lord Somers (1651-1716) 1706

Bust

20.5 (8)

The National Trust, Wimpole Hall, Cambridgeshire (purchased with the assistance of the National Art-Collections Fund)

Condition: good

Inscr: (on the back) D LE MARCHAND Sculp. A. 1706

PROV: Lord Somers, 1706 (presented by him to Lord Halifax?); Lord Halifax (sold Cocks, Covent Garden 1739); Edward Harley, 2nd Earl of Oxford (1689-1741), (bought 1739 and taken to Wimpole Hall); Inherited by his widow, the Countess of Oxford (sold 1742); bought by Philip Yorke, 1st Earl of Hardwicke, their nephew, and returned to

Wimpole Hall; By descent to Lord Clifden at Wimpole Hall until 1938; (Wimpole Hall sold to Captain & Mrs George Bambridge); Acquired by Sir Albert Richardson (d.1967); Lady Richardson (d.1984); Accepted by the Capital Taxes Office in lieu of tax and placed at Wimpole Hall (1985)

LIT: Chennevières-Pointel, 1857, p.12; Dussieux, 1876, p.273; Maze-Sencier, 1885, p.639; Lami, 1906, p.317; Vertue, IV, p.166; Longhurst, 1926, p.59; Houfe, 1971, pp.68-9, fig.4; S. Houfe, 1980, pp.151-2; Avery, 1984, p.113; The National Trust, *Wimpole Hall*, London, 1985, p.18

Vertue described what must be this bust among the 'Pictures sold in Lord Halifax's sale': 'Earl of Oxford bought a head a small bust in Ivory of Ld Sommers with a large Wigg – done from the life cutt by D. Le Marchand 1706'. The last part of this information was presumably derived from reading the inscription on its back. Lord Somers was twice portrayed by Sir Godfrey Kneller in the same span of years (National Portrait Gallery, nos 490, 3223; ill.).

Somers is described as follows in the catalogue of the National Portrait Gallery: 'Politician. Educated at Trinity College, Oxford, he entered the Middle Temple in 1669 and, having won a great legal reputation, was junior counsel for the Seven Bishops in 1688. He helped to draft the Bill of Rights; as Solicitor-General and Attorney-General he created a new and important tradition by his temperate prosecution of the enemies of the new régime of William and Mary; as a leader of the Whigs he organised the Junto, a close body of ministers which in some ways anticipated the Cabinet. He became a Baron and Lord Chancellor (1697), but a Tory House tried to impeach him in 1700. He held office under Anne from 1708 to 1710, but the queen did not like him, and he went out of office when the Tories came in. He was described as a "man of broad intellectual power and weighty in the law". Swift thought he "possessed all excellent qualifications, except virtue". Somers was a considerable patron of the arts, and a much-painted sitter.'

Le Marchand's bust, according to Houfe, 'shows the Chancellor at the age of fifty-five at the close of his career. In 1706, the year it was carved,

Somers had been virtual leader of the Whig party for four years since the accession of Queen Anne. During this time he had been out of office and it is possible that he and his friend Lord Halifax wished to commemorate past triumphs together by giving each other presents. This accounts for the bust being in Lord Halifax's collection and suggests that much of Le Marchand's work may have been of a presentation or official nature.'

Houfe continues: 'Addison was to record in *The Freeholder*, no.39, at Somer's death that "his opinion of a piece of poetry, a statue or a picture . . . was so just and delicate as naturally produced pleasure and assent in those who heard him." Dean Swift who was predictably enough first his ally, later his enemy, dedicated *A Tale of a Tub* to him in 1704. Somers was also among the first to patronise George Vertue as an engraver.'

Houfe, 1980, tells the story of his grandfather's acquisition of the bust in 1941 from an antique dealer in Cambridge.

38* (Plate 3)
John Vesey, Archbishop of Tuam (1638-1716) 1702
Bust
28 (11) overall
Private Collection
Condition: slight cracking; break at bottom of ecclesiastical collar
Inscr: (on the reverse) Jon. Vesey / ArchBisp. / of Tuam / An. Do. / 1702 / AEt. Su. / 65 / Le March. f.

PROV: By family descent

John Vesey, Archbishop of Tuam, also sat for a painted portrait, while a marble bust similar to Le Marchand's portrait also exists.

Educated at Westminster School, and an MA of Trinity College, Dublin, he received his Doctorate of Divinity in 1672. He was appointed Archdeacon of Armagh 1662-3, Dean of Cork Cathedral in 1667, Bishop of Limerick in 1673 and Archbishop of Tuam in 1678. He was also Warden of Galway.

37

Sir Godfrey Kneller Bt, *Baron Somers*, National Portrait Gallery, London (3223).

38

In 1689, in a reaction against the Glorious Revolution, his palace in Tuam was burned down by a Catholic Jacobite mob, and he sailed for England under hot pursuit. Safely in London, he had to maintain himself with a Readership in St Paul's Cathedral of a paltry ten shillings per annum, but later was able to return to Ireland, in 1692, after which his circumstances returned to a normal degree of prosperity. This would have enabled him to commission in 1702 an expensive item like this ivory bust.

39
Sir Godfrey Kneller (?1646-1723) 1700-10
Portrait medallion; profile to the right
12.5 (5)
Collection of Lord Thomson of Fleet, Toronto
Condition: perfect

PROV: With Cyril Humphris, London, 1978

The identification is based on the close similarity of this medallic profile with that on a circular medallion showing Godfrey Kneller as Principal Painter to the King of Great Britain that was initialled and dated 1688 on the reverse by Jean Cavalier.[1]

If the connection of Le Marchand's subject is correct, it would be another case where both carvers depicted the same subject, as with the diarist Pepys (Cat.40). David's bust of Locke is also closely connected with Kneller's portrait of 1697 (Cat.69), and their respective portraits of Newton and of Stukeley (Cats 44, 54) are intimately related. Indeed there are enough points of contact to suggest that they may have been friends as well as colleagues, with David possibly succeeding his French predecessor, Cavalier, after 1699 in Kneller's confidence. They shared the favours of many of the same, influential sitters, such as Somers (Cat.37).

Sir Godfrey Kneller was born in Lübeck, studied under Bol in Amsterdam, and then went to Italy, where Maratta influenced his work. He settled in England in 1674, gaining introduction to Court circles through Monmouth, c.1677. By c.1685 he was becoming the most fashionable painter; appointed Principal Painter (with Riley) at the Revolution, he was knighted in 1692, and created a Baronet in 1715.

Kneller's production was immense, and his large team of assistants formed virtually a factory; the standard product was rather mechanical and lifeless, yet Kneller's individual masterpieces rank as high as any portraits produced in Europe in his time. By c.1685 his true style was formed, and is at its best crisper, cleaner and more vigorous than Lely's.

1 National Portrait Gallery, London, no.1740: 3¾ inch diam, inscribed GOTHOFRIDVS. KNELLER. PRIM. PICT. REGIS. MAG. BRITANIAE. and initialled I.C. (D. Piper, *Seventeenth Century Portraits in the National Portrait Gallery*, Cambridge, 1963, p.191)

40* (Plate 12)
Samuel Pepys (1633-1703) 1700-05
Portrait medallion; profile to the right
13.2 × 10.6 $(5\frac{3}{16} \times 4\frac{1}{8})$
The British Museum, London, No.458
Condition: slightly discoloured
Inscr: (on the ground beneath the truncation of the shoulder) D.L.M.F.

PROV: A.W. Franks; presented to the British Museum, 1884

LIT: Maskell, 1905, pl.LXVI; Dalton, 1909, no.458, p.152; Longhurst, 1926, p.60; Museum of London, 1985, no.304, p.208

39

Jean Cavalier, *Samuel Pepys*, ivory, 1688,
Clothworkers' Company, London.

41

There is another medallion of the diarist (profile also to the right) by Jean Cavalier, carved in 1688, which now belongs to the Clothworkers' Company (ill.p.74).[1] Pepys had unfortunately ceased to keep up his famous diary by that date, so that one has no idea whether, as seems likely, he commissioned Cavalier, let alone Le Marchand, personally. Pepys had been elected Governor of St Thomas's Hospital on 1 August 1684, but was not a regular attender at meetings.[2] This would have brought Pepys, albeit at the very end of his days, into contact with a number of Le Marchand's other patrons, after the carver's arrival in London, c.1700. Pepys died soon afterwards, and so the portrait may be a posthumous memento, worked up by David from Cavalier's earlier medallion, for a third party who admired its subject.

A comparison of the two points up the differences of approach, as between the dry, incisive, medallic quality of Cavalier, and the more boldly sculptural treatment of draped shoulders, fleshy facial features and the luxuriant curls of the wig, that characterise Le Marchand.

1 I am most grateful to Mr D. E. Wickham, Archivist of the Clothworkers' Company, for allowing the British Museum to take a photograph and for giving permission to reproduce it here
2 My thanks to Peter Edden for this observation (see Cat.42, note 1)

41*

John Locke (1632-1704) Date unknown
Oval portrait medallion; in profile to the right
11.4 (4½)
Private Collection, London
Condition: perfect

PROV: The Weld-Blundell family, of Ince Blundell, Lancashire (sold Christie's, 13 December 1994, lot 30)

LIT: Avery, 1984, pp.113-18, pls XVII-XX; Avery, 1985, pp.1562-4
[Both repr. in Avery, 1987, pp.241-52]

David le Marchand carved and signed a handsome bust (21.5 cm; 8½ in high) of John Locke (1632-1704) when Locke was sixty-five (Cat.69). The bust is known only from photographs taken when it was brought to the Victoria & Albert Museum for opinion in 1936. The profile view is virtually identical to the present medallic image, which is probably a derivative from the commission for the bust.

Particularly significant is the quiff of hair drawn back over Locke's forehead, while the sinuous curves of the waxy-looking folds of drapery round the truncation are characteristic of Le Marchand's style. The absence of his initials, D.L.M., found on some medallions is not significant, for by no means all are signed.

42* (Plate 15)

After a wax model perhaps by François Le Pipre (1640-1698)
Thomas Guy (1645-1724) 1700-26
Rectangular portrait plaque; full-frontal
20.5 × 13.5 (8 × 5⅜)
The Victoria & Albert Museum, London, A.1-1936
Condition: excellent
Inscr: (on the reverse) D.L.M. sculp.

PROV: 'Sale in London' (see Eason, loc.cit.); Given by Dr W. L. Hildburgh FSA

LIT: S. Wilks and G. T. Bettany, *A Biographical History of Guy's Hospital*, London, 1892; H. L. Eason, 'A New Portrait of Thomas Guy', in *Guy's Hospital Gazette*, New Series, April 1936, pp.149-51; Victoria & Albert Museum, *Review*, 1936, pp.2, 3, pl.3(a); H. C. Cameron, *Mr. Guy's Hospital*, London, 1954 (1965); Hodgkinson, 1965, p.29, fig.3; Avery, 1984, p.113

Other example: see Cat.43

Thomas Guy is famous as the founder of Guy's Hospital, London. A bookseller by profession, received into the Livery of the Stationers' Company in 1673, Guy flourished mightily. His early prosperity enabled him to build an almshouse (1678) and subscribe to a charity school (1687) in his native Tamworth, becoming its MP in 1695.[1] He soon expanded the almshouse and financed a new Town Hall in 1701, marking his gift with a coat-of-arms that he 'borrowed' from the family Guy of Oundle, Northamptonshire. In 1707 Thomas and his brother joined the governing body of St Thomas's Hospital, building new wards and assisting with administration, for the ensuing decade and a half.

Mr Guy continued living at the Oxford Arms in Lombard Street, the financial centre of the day, and hence became involved with investing in the nascent Bank of England, as well as in the South Sea Company (from 1711). These activities would have brought him into contact with some of Le Marchand's best patrons, such as the Rapers, who were Directors and Governors (Cats 62, 65). Unlike the mathematician and scientist Sir Isaac Newton, who lost £20,000 in the South Sea Bubble of 1720, a speculative investment fiasco of vast proportions, Guy shrewdly divested himself of the stock at a huge profit just before the event, gaining a fortune of £160,000 – well over one million pounds in today's debased currency.[2]

This made him overnight 'seriously rich' and he was influenced by a close medical friend, Dr Richard Mead, to devote a sizeable proportion – if not all – of it to founding a new hospital in his own name. Both were Governors of St Thomas's Hospital on its old site near London Bridge (now overshadowed by the elevated railway, and abandoned long since for Lambeth) and Guy's foundation was to be opposite it. Though much altered and added to, the old building round a double courtyard, with wards for four hundred patients, is still readily discernible. Its founder died in 1724 just as workmen were putting the finishing touches to his hospital.

Apart from the amazing personal generosity involved, its dedication to the poorest and sickest of the poor – the 'incurables' – in the urban squalor of old London town make it remarkable. Guy's legendary reputation for stinginess may have some foundation, but it was designed to serve a good and noble end, which should stay the pens of denigrators. He was not only abstemious but self-effacing, and at his death owned no portraits of himself.

It is therefore unlikely that he commissioned Le Marchand. He was however in close touch through the Boards of Governors of St Thomas's and his own hospital with a number of patrons of the ivory carver. For instance he knew Sir Isaac Newton and Dr Mead, who owned David's plaque from life of Newton, as well as some medallions of Roman emperors.

Another prominent patron, Moses Raper (Cat.65), a friend of the artist, gave an operating theatre to Guy's Hospital after the founder's death, in 1739, and he is therefore a likely candidate as instigator of the carving in ivory of this impressive image, thus rendering more magnificent (on account of the luxury material) and permanent the striking full-face portrait modelled in wax apparently by Le Pipre before his death in 1698. Thereafter, the date of carving is uncertain and may be from as early as c.1700, or as late as to follow Guy's death in 1724, for the carver outlived him by two years and was still carving very well in 1722, when he portrayed the Reverend William Stukeley (Cat.54).

The relationship of this ivory carving with the wax image is revealing (Cat.43). The wax is slightly larger than the ivory, and so cannot have been cast from it, and it may indeed be a preliminary model, taken from life. The issue is further complicated by the existence of an engraving (Cat.43) showing the wax version and inscribed 'From a model in wax by his friend F. Le Pipre'. The obvious inference is that Le Marchand was employed simply to copy the wax, and thus render the image more durable, and this he could have done at any time up until his death in 1726.

Le Marchand used the same, frontal, pose to good effect on one other portrait, the plaque of Sir Isaac Newton (Cat.44). Indeed, their similarity tempts one to speculate as to whether the wax image now in Corsham Court might not also be by Le Pipre (Cat.45).

1 I am most grateful to Mr Peter Edden of Tamworth for allowing me to read an unpublished manuscript of his book on Mr Guy. This and further discussions and correspondence have been an invaluable help in 'historically situating' the wax model perhaps by Le Pipre and the ivory portrait by Le Marchand
2 I understand that a factor of around seventy is used today in the Bank of England to convert eighteenth-century currency into its modern equivalent

43*
Perhaps by François Le Pipre (1640-1698)
Thomas Guy (1645-1724) Before 1698
Wax portrait relief; full-frontal
27 × 21.5 (10$\frac{1}{8}$ × 8$\frac{1}{2}$)
Guy's Hospital, The Gordon Museum, London
Condition: chipping and damage to right shoulder

PROV: Benjamin Harrison Jr, Treasurer of Guy's Hospital 1797-1848 (whose sister married into the Cripps family); By family descent to Sir Frederick Cripps (his sale, Cirencester, 1960, p.21, lot 418: 'A wax carving of J. Guy, Esq. *(founder of Guy's Hospital)* on a black slate base under glass shade.'; Frost and Reed (sold to the hospital 1960)

LIT: E. J. Pyke, *A Biographical Dictionary of Wax Modellers*, Oxford, 1973, p.79 (Le Pipre: this model not listed); H. L. Eason, in *Guy's Hospital Gazette*, New Series, April 1936, pp.149-51

For discussion, see Cat.42

An old but certainly misleading inscription on the back of the frame of the wax indicated that it was modelled after a death mask by Gosset: 'Conceived to have been modelled from a cast taken after death by Mr. Gosset, father of the late Dr. Gosset, of Book Auction celebrity, Mr. Gosset having been an able artist in that way about the time of Guy's death.' This is impossible, but it was reproduced with a misleading caption in *The Connoisseur*, CXLV, May 1960, p.277.

The inscription under the old engraving that ascribes it to Le Pipre seems perfectly reliable: the information it gives is so unexpected that it

is unlikely to have been invented. François Le Pipre (or Piper) was a painter of portraits in the style of Hogarth, of whom it was written in 1706 (Buckridge, *An Essay Towards An English School*): 'in the latter part of his life [Le Pipre] applied himself to the Study and Practice of Modelling in wax, in *basso-rilievo*, in which he did abundance of things with good success. He often said he wished he had thought of it sooner, for that sort of work suited better with his genius than any. Had he lived longer he would have arrived to a great Perfection in it.'

Possibly Le Marchand was led by the example of Le Pipre to model his portraits in wax, before carving them in ivory, and this may have led to the distinctly 'waxy' appearance of his idiosyncratic treatment of drapery and hair, that emerged only after his arrival in London c.1700.

44* (Plate 14)
Sir Isaac Newton PRS (1642-1727) 1702-10
Rectangular portrait plaque; full-frontal in high relief
19.75 × 13 (7$\frac{3}{4}$ × 5$\frac{1}{8}$)
Collection of Lord Thomson of Fleet, Toronto
Condition: excellent
Inscr: D. Le Marchad [*sic*] ad Viv. Sc.lt

PROV: Dr Richard Mead MD (sold 11 March 1755 by A. Langford in association with Samuel Baker in *The Musei Meadiani Pars Prior Sale*);[1] [Edward Poore Esq., deceased (sale Richardson's, 31 The Strand, London, 19 April 1805, lot 49: for discussion, see our Cat.46) (?)]; Sotheby's, 20 December 1963, lot 165

LIT: Vertue, II, pp.69-70; Reilly and Savage, 1973, p.257; Westfall, 1980, pp.759, 854; Avery, 1985, p.1564, fig.9; Gjertsen, 1986, p.444, *Busts*, no.2

Other examples: see Cat.46, and a framed oval medallion in black basalt by Wedgwood and Bentley, Wedgwood Museum, Barlaston

The present relief was described by Vertue, who mentions three portraits of Newton, as 'an Alto-relieve with the wigg on . . . by Marchand this last I think the best & in poses Dr. Meade'.

Of at least four prime images of Newton by Le Marchand – two plaques showing him in a wig (see Cat.46) and two busts showing his own hair, dated 1714 and 1718 (Cats 47,68) – the present one most closely resembles the portrait painted by Kneller of 1702 (National Portrait Gallery, London, no.2881) and a more formal one by Jervas of 1703 (Royal Society, London), the latter occasioned by Isaac's election as President of the Royal Society (Westfall, 1980, figs 12.2 and 13.1).

It is indeed possible that Le Marchand was present at the sittings given to Kneller in 1702, for the painter liked to keep his subjects in lively conversation, as one knows from an account by Stukeley of a sitting of Newton's in 1720, at which he was invited by both to be present (Westfall, 1980, p.851). The studied casualness of the open-necked shirt, implying an intellectual disdain for obvious signs of worldly importance, is common to all of Kneller's and Le Marchand's representations of Sir Isaac, even after his knighthood.

After an academic career at Trinity College, Cambridge, during which he made most of his important mathematical and scientific discoveries, Newton was appointed Warden of the Royal Mint in 1696 at the suggestion of Charles Montagu, a former protégé and then Chancellor of the Exchequer.[2] Montagu was also involved in the establishment of the

Bank of England (see p.23). Newton took up office in the Tower of London at a moment when the Mint was attempting to rationalise the coinage of the realm, and to defeat counterfeiters. In 1699 he accepted the more lucrative post of Master of the Mint and continued in office for the remaining thirty years of his life. Early on he had to make coins and coronation medals for Queen Anne's accession (1702) and later for that of George I (1714).

Isaac Newton was elected President of the Royal Society in 1702, and he was a Governor of Christ's Hospital, nominating Thomas Guy (Cat.42) as a Governor in 1709, but Guy declined, though he left an endowment at Christ's in his will.

The first recorded owner of the plaque, Dr Richard Mead (1673-1754),[3] attended Sir Isaac Newton as well as George I and George II, Sir Robert Walpole and Bishop Burnet. He was on the Council of the Royal Society in 1705 and 1707-54 and was Vice-president in 1717. He collected objects of vertu and financially assisted various literary projects. In 1702 he published a 'Mechanical Account of Poisons' (an account of venomous snakes), and two years later a treatise on the influence of the sun and moon on human bodies.

The ivory bust of Newton in the round, also by Le Marchand (Cat.68), in the British Museum, *Catalogue of Ivory Carvings*, p.151, no.455, was wrongly identified as that in the collection of Dr Mead in 1755.

1 The relief was described on p.253: 'ISAACI NEWTONI equitis aurati protome, pleno ore, ad dimidium exstans: a *D.L. Marchand* ad vivum sculpta. *Alt. septem uncias cum semisse, lat. quinque.*' (£5.5.0) It is worth noting that the measurements of the present relief correspond with those given in the Catalogue of the Mead sale
2 See *Isaac Newton at the Royal Mint*, exh.cat., Royal Mint and Bank of England, London, 1992
3 *Country Life*, 29 January 1970

45*
Sir Isaac Newton PRS (1642-1727) 1702-10
Wax, full-frontal, high-relief portrait
15.2 (6)
Trustees of the Corsham Estate, Corsham Court, Wiltshire
Condition: slight cracking on the wax relief itself; some damage to background
Other examples: see Cats 44, 46

This is either the model for, or a cast of, the Newton relief in Dr Mead's sale (Cat.44).

46
Sir Isaac Newton PRS (1642-1727) 1702-10
Portrait medallion; three-quarter profile to the left
24.2×20.4 ($9\frac{1}{2} \times 8$)
Lost
Condition: good

PROV: J. W. Brett sale, Christie's, 5 April 1864, lot 2035: 'An alto-relievo bust of Sir Isaac Newton, by Denis [*sic*] Le Marchand, in a black frame – oval – $9\frac{1}{2}$ in by 8 in'; Purchased by Bohn (£7.15s)

LIT: Avery, 1985, p.1564, fig.8

Other example: see Cat.44

The firmly modelled jaw of Newton and the cleverly foreshortened head in this difficult three-quarter portrait betray Le Marchand's expertise, while the handling of the periwig and waxy-looking folds of drapery round the truncation of the bust are characteristic.

43

45

46

The fact that the item was illustrated in such an early Christie's catalogue indicates its importance, and the mistake in the carver's name suggests that it was perhaps just initialled 'D.L.M.' and the cataloguer remembered the carver's christian name incorrectly. This excellent medallion has not been seen for well over a century.

A portrait of broadly similar description had appeared in an early-nineteenth-century sale catalogue, *Prints and Drawings . . . of the late Edward Poore, Esq., Deceased*, at Richardson's, 31 The Strand, London, Friday April 19, 1805, lot 49: 'Sir Isaac Newton, a Bust in ivory by D.L.M., very fine, framed and glazed'. The latter part of this entry suggests that the 'bust', which realised £4, was in relief, for a free-standing bust could hardly be described as framed and glazed. This relief may be identical either with the present one, which reappeared at Christie's in 1864; or with the more famous relief of Newton, showing him full-face, in periwig and half-length, which had once belonged to the celebrated Dr Richard Mead (Cat.44).

47 (Plate 10)
Sir Isaac Newton PRS (1642-1727) 1714
Bust
18.6 × 13.3 × 8.8 (7⅞ × 5¼ × 3½)
National Gallery of Victoria, Melbourne, Australia (4118.3)
Condition: ivory discoloured and slightly cracked
Inscr: (on back of small, cylindrical marble stand) D.L.M.Sct. 1714

PROV: Lord Halifax (sold Cocks, Covent Garden, 1739); 2nd Earl of Oxford (1689-1741), Wimpole Hall, Cambs. (bought as above); [James West, PRS (sale, Langford & Son, London, 6 March 1773, p.22, lot 19) ?]; Countess of Gosford, 1930s; With Alfred Spero, London; Howard Spensley, Westoning Manor, Bedfordshire (bought from Spero for £30); Bequeathed to the National Art Collections-Fund, to be presented to the Government of Victoria, in 1939

LIT: Vertue, IV, p.166; National Gallery of Victoria, *Catalogue of the Howard Spensley Bequest*, Melbourne, c.1939, no.213; Westfall, 1980, p.854; Gjertsen, 1986, p.444, *Busts*, no.1 (without giving date or location)

Other examples: see Cats 68, 69b, 69d

Vertue describes a bust that, given the inscribed date, must be identical with this one among the 'Pictures sold in Lord Halifax's sale': 'dito. a small bust in Ivory done from the life Sir Isaac Newton a head without a wigg – 1714 by Marchand'. The absence of the wig gives an almost modern look to this trenchant portrait.

Presumably commissioned, or acquired, by Lord Halifax, the bust *may* be identical with one that later in the eighteenth century featured in the sale of the estate of James West in 1773, described as: 'a small ivory bust of Sir Isaac Newton on a stone pedestal'. The latter element may well be the one on which the bust still stands in Australia. The donor, who acquired the bust in London, came originally from Melbourne.

48*
Sir Christopher Wren (1632-1723) 1700-20
Portrait medallion; profile to the right
12.2 × 9.4 (5 × 3⅝)
The National Portrait Gallery, London, No.4500

Condition: An old damage at the back of the wig has been restored in wax since its purchase by the National Portrait Gallery.
Unsigned, but on a nineteenth-century label attached to the back of the frame is the inscription: BUST of/ Sir Christopher Wren/ Architect/ Born Oct. 20, 1633/ Died 1724 [*sic*]/ aged 91 years/ In ivory by/ Denis le Marchant/ for my dear daughter/ Margaret. H. Willett.

PROV: [Mr. Willet, c.1763?]; [Henry Willett, Brighton (?)]; Margaret H. Willett, c.1880; Mrs Vasey until c.1940; S.R. Hawkswell; Sotheby's, 4 July 1966, lot 54 (bought by David Peel, £420); Purchased by the National Portrait Gallery, October 1966

EXH: Museum of London, 1985, no.310

LIT: *Walpole* (ed. R. N. Wornum), 1849, II, p.625; National Portrait Gallery, *Annual Report of the Trustees*, HMSO, 1967, pp.32-3, no.4500; Houfe, 1971, pp.67, 69, fig.3; K. K. Yung, *Complete Illustrated Catalogue*, National Portrait Gallery, 1981, p.627

Other example: see Cat.67

The old ink inscription on the back of the frame implies that the medallion once belonged to a Mr Willett. Vertue noted that a 'Mr. Willet has another head of a gentleman, pretty large, with the initial letters, D.L.M.'. As the present portrait is *not* initialled, Vertue may have been conflating it with the relief of Wren's son, Christopher (Cat.49), which *is* so initialled, and which Willet may also have owned. Though not a facing pair, nor the same size, the reliefs are linked by their sitters' familial relationship, and may always have been together, for they eventually appeared in the same sale at Sotheby's, and were from the same property.

47

The medallion was engraved, in reverse, by S. Coignand as 'after a bust' for Christopher Wren, Jr, *Parentalia*, published by Stephen Wren in 1750. It was reproduced as a Wedgwood medallion in 1773, for which the original plaster mould survives at Barlaston.

This portrait was done towards the end of Wren's life, but has an '*ad vivum*' quality. Though unsigned, it seems to have been associated with the signed medallion showing his son, and may certainly be counted among the autograph works of Le Marchand. It served as a model for Gaab's later bronze medal of Wren (ill.).

49*
Christopher Wren (Junior) Esq MP (1675-1747) 1700-20
Portrait medallion; profile to the right
11.5 (4½)
Collection of Lord Thomson of Fleet, Toronto
Condition: good
Inscr: (on the ground under the truncation) D.L.M.

PROV: [Mr. Willet, *c*.1763?]; [Henry Willett, Brighton (?)]; Margaret H. Willett (his daughter); Mrs Vasey until *c*.1940; S.R. Hawkswell; Sotheby's, 4 July 1966, lot 55

LIT: *Walpole* (ed. R. N. Wornum), 1849, II, p.625; National Portrait Gallery, *Annual Report of the Trustees*, HMSO, 1967, pp.33

This relief was sold by Sotheby's as the succeeding lot and near-pair to the unsigned medallion of Sir Christopher Wren (Cat.48). It was incorrectly identified in their catalogue as the Duke of Marlborough, but as pointed out in the *Annual Report* of the National Portrait Gallery, it 'bore a similar and perfectly plausible inscription on the back identifying the sitter as Christopher Wren Jr.'. This portrait is presumably the one commented on by Vertue: 'Mr. Willett has another head of a gentleman, pretty large, with the initial letters, D.L.M.'.

Son of Sir Christopher, the architect, Christopher Jr collected documents about him which form the *Parentalia*, 1750. He was educated at Eton College and Pembroke Hall, Cambridge. His election as MP for Windsor in 1713 might have occasioned this portrait, when he was thirty-eight, an age consistent with his appearance in Le Marchand's profile.

50*
Charles Marbury (Life dates not known) 1700-20
Portrait medallion; profile to the right
12.7 × 9.5 (5 × 3¾)
Collection Herr Reiner Winkler, Wiesbaden
Condition: tip of nose replaced, otherwise excellent

PROV: With Mr Pierce of Nottingham (Antique Dealer); A. Bower Esq, Matlock, Derbyshire; Sotheby's, 21 April 1988, lot 296 (unsold)

LIT: Vertue, IV, p.50; *Walpole* (ed. R. N. Wornum), 1849, II, p.625; Theuerkauff, 1994, pp.58-59, no.20

Other example: see Cat.51

The profile was formerly set on glass with a black paper backing, which was replaced with perspex by the previous owner, Mr Bower. That mount was presumably itself a replacement when the original mirror-glass became dulled or broken. The reflective glass background accords with the description by Vertue of 'a profil head in Ivory, sett on a looking glass carvd by David Le Merchand. its the portrait as written

G. D. Gaab, *Sir Christopher Wren*, bronze medal, private collection.

49

48

underneath – Charles Marbury. Generallissimo of the Society della Rosa. and grand Master of all Arts & Sciences, in ye time of K. Ch. 2d. and King James.' The italianate 'title' (bestowed for amusement's sake) that Vertue recorded, no doubt refers to the artistic and antiquarian Rose and Crown Club.[1] It was assumed, until recently, that this description referred to the profile of Marbury in the Victoria & Albert Museum (Cat.51), yet the background of that is carved out of ivory, and so it cannot be the example described by Vertue.

Charles was probably a member of the Marbury family of Marbury Hall, near Comerback in Cheshire, the last recorded male heir of which died in 1684 (G. Ormerod, *History of Cheshire*, I, London, 1882, pp.635-7). The estate passed in 1708 by marriage to Earl Rivers and was eventually sold by auction in 1933.

Though unsigned, the medallion is unmistakably in the mature style of Le Marchand, and the sitter is identical (save for the restored nose) to that in the oval ivory medallion in the Victoria & Albert Museum, which is initialled and said to represent Marbury in an inscription on an old paper label on its reverse. However, as Theuerkauff notes, the techniques are slightly different: the curls of the wig in the present carving are more luxuriant, and their tips are emphasised by a drill-hole in each. There is also an area of straighter hair over the nape of the neck and the curls tumble down the back and over the shoulder blades, while other curls flow over the mantle beside the neck. In the other version, perhaps the earlier because it seems to be the simpler of the two, the curls of the wig are combed backwards in waves, there is no plain area behind and the ones falling down over the clavicle are encompassed by the cloak.

1 U. & L. Lippincott, *Selling Art in Georgian London*, New Haven/London, 1983, pp.16, 30, 170, n.29

51★
Charles Marbury (Life dates not known) 1700-20
Portrait medallion; profile to the right
13×9 ($5 \times 3\frac{1}{2}$)
The Victoria & Albert Museum, London, A.43-1931
Condition: excellent
Inscr: (on the ground below the truncation) D.L.M.

PROV: (According to an inscription on the back of the old frame, written in late 18th- or early 19th-century hand): Sir James Lowther; The Reverend E. Chappelowe; Mrs Mason (? in 1773)

LIT: Chennevières-Pointel, 1857, p.12; Dussieux, 1876, p.273; Maze-Sencier, 1885, p.639; Lami, 1906, p.317

Other example: see Cat.50

On an oval-shaped label fixed to the back were seven lines of verse, partly defaced, subscribed E.R. and prefaced there as follows: 'These Verses (suppos'd to be written by a Lady of Quality) were . . . fixt to Mr. Marbury's picture drawn by Mr. Closterman.'

For discussion see Cat.50

52★
John Flamsteed (1646-1719) 1719
Portrait medallion; profile to the right
12.1×9.8 ($4\frac{3}{4} \times 3\frac{7}{8}$)
The Royal Greenwich Observatory, Cambridge
Condition: good
Inscr: (on the ground below the truncation of the shoulder) D.L.M.; (on the reverse) IOH; FLAMSTEDIVS/Math. Reg./ AEtat. An. 73 completo/ 1719

PROV: Presented to the Royal Observatory by John Belchier FRS, at some time between the visitations of the Royal Observatory on 10 July 1776

50   51   52

and 2 June 1777. On the latter date it was noted that a recent gift, then in the dwelling-house (*ie* the residence of the Astronomer Royal, Nevil Maskelyne) was to be added to the inventory, *viz*, 'an alto Relievo Ivory carving of Flamsteed's head by Marchand, presented to the Royal Observatory by Mr. Belchier'.

LIT: Longhurst, 1926, p.59; P. S. Laurie, *The Old Royal Observatory*, National Maritime Museum, Department of Navigation and Astronomy, 1960, pp.3-8

John Flamsteed, a young Derbyshire clergyman whose astronomical and mathematical ability was already becoming known, was appointed to the position of the first Astronomer Royal in 1675, which he held until his death in 1719, the year of this medallion.

John Belchier (1706-85), an eminent surgeon, was elected FRS in 1723; he served on the Council of the Royal Society from 1769-72 and 1776-9 (at the time of the gift).

53*
Sir Richard Steele MP (1672-1729) *c*.1715
Portrait medallion cast in steel; profile to the right
$7.1 \times 5.4 \left(2\frac{3}{4} \times 2\frac{1}{8}\right)$
The British Museum, London, Department of Coins and Medals
(M.8277)

LIT: Franks and Gruber, 1885/1904/11, pl.CL, 5

The style of the drapery round the truncation, the firm profile and the treatment of the wig resemble those of Le Marchand. The unusual material was presumably chosen as a punning reference to the subject's surname. It could have been cast from a wax model such as Le Marchand customarily made, instead of being carved from ivory.

If it is by Le Marchand, it must have been carved in the early 1720s,

53

when the sitter was about fifty years old, rather than at the time of his death, as suggested by Franks and Gruber, for that occurred three years after Le Marchand's demise.

Sir Richard Steele, author and politician, was educated at Charterhouse and at Merton College, Oxford. At an early stage he displayed a talent for dramatic composition, but it was not till 1701 that his first successful comedy, *The Funeral, or Grief à la Mode*, was produced. His most important writings, in conjunction with Addison, were in the *Tatler*, which he founded in 1709; *The Spectator*, begun in 1711, and the *Guardian*, first published in 1713.

Steele was elected MP for Stockbridge in 1713, but was expelled from the House for seditious libel in March of the following year. On the accession of the House of Hanover he received the lucrative sinecure of Surveyor to the Royal Stables of Hampton Court, and was again returned to Parliament as Member for Boroughbridge in 1715. He received the honour of knighthood in the same year. He also established the 'Sensorium' or 'Censorium' Club.

The present profile is consistent with the full-face portrait painted by Kneller, which shows the squarish shape of face with pointed nose and chin (H. Paul, *Queen Anne*, London, 1906, pl. opp. p.114).

54*
The Reverend William Stukeley MD FRS FSA (1687-1765) 1722
Portrait medallion; profile to the right
$9.8 \times 7.8 \left(3\frac{7}{8} \times 3\frac{1}{16}\right)$
Collection of Michael Hall Esq, London
Condition: excellent
Inscr: (on the reverse) W. STVKELEY
On a paper label at one time glued to the back of the ivory medallion there is printed a coat-of-arms: that of the St John family, who were related by marriage to the Stukeleys.

PROV: William Stukeley MD; By family descent to The Reverend H. F. St John (*c*.1880), Dinmore House, nr Leominster;[1] By family descent

LIT: 'The Family Memoirs of the Rev. William Stukeley, MD', in *The Surtees Society*, 73, London, 1882, I, pp.67, 131

Other example: pewter cast in Wedgwood Museum, Barlaston (No.3081: $9.7 \times 7.7 \left(3\frac{13}{16} \times 3\frac{7}{16}\right)$); cast in Wedgwood black basalt, British Museum

This medallion of the Reverend William Stukeley, the early English archaeologist and founder-member of the Society of Antiquaries, is the only known example by Le Marchand of a wreathed head in classical guise. This was almost certainly imposed upon Le Marchand by the sitter. Though the piece is unsigned, its subject's name is inscribed on the verso in Le Marchand's bold but uneven hand, and the sitting was actually recorded in Stukeley's *Family Memoirs* for 11 July 1722: 'I sat to Mr. Marchand cutting my Profile in basso rilievo in Ivory'. It is the only ivory for which an actual sitting is recorded, and is at present David Le Marchand's last datable work. Stukeley had sat for his portrait to Kneller only the year before and a fine drawing in pencil, ink and wash inscribed and dated 1721 survives in the National Portrait Gallery (no.4266; ill.p.82). Le Marchand's medallic profile of Stukeley faces to the right as well, and seems to be indebted to Kneller's interpretation of their mutual sitter.

In June 1726 Stukeley noted the death of one among his most

intimate friends in London, 'the famous cutter in ivory Monsr. Marchand, who cut my profile'.[2]

Stukeley read medicine at Corpus Christi College, Cambridge (1703-8), and then went to London in 1718, joining the Royal Society, where he soon met Sir Isaac Newton. Both came from Lincolnshire. When Stukeley returned to his native Grantham in 1726, having exhausted the possibility of the metropolis and depressed by the deaths of so many of his close friends, including Newton and Le Marchand, he went about collecting all the information he could on Sir Isaac: indeed much of what one knows of Newton's later years are due to Stukeley's diligence and recording of his own experiences.[3]

As Professor Westfall writes: 'Stukeley had the good fortune, at the request of both men involved, to attend all the sittings when Sir Godfrey Kneller painted Newton for Varignon in 1720'. Stukeley himself described the occasion: 'Tho' it was Sir Isaac's temper to say little yet it was one of Sir Godfrys arts to keep up a perpetual discourse, to preserve the lines and spirit of a face. I was delighted to observe Sir Godfry, who was not famous for sentiments of religion, sifting Sir Isaac to find out his notions on that head, who answered him with his usual modesty and caution.' Westfall continues: 'Stukeley asked Newton to let Kneller do a profile of him; "what says Sir Isaac, would you make a medal of me? and refused it, tho' I was then in highest favour with him". Nevertheless, at some time or other, Stukeley, who was something of an amateur artist, sketched a profile of Newton for himself.'

The drawing is preserved in the Royal Society, and is signed and inscribed 'ad vivum fecit', ie 'from life'. An allegorical polymast female figure, seated on a celestial globe with the constellation of the Plough clearly indicated, supports a disproportionately large circular medallion. This shows Newton in profile to the right, his ageing, drawn features creditably delineated in chiaroscuro, and with his own short hair (curled to suit the classicising imagery) bound by a fillet.

Not only does this strongly resemble the portrait of Stukeley created for him in 1722 by the more accomplished hand of Le Marchand, but both seem to betray a knowledge of another medallion carved in ivory by G. B. Pozzo at Rome in 1717 depicting another distinguished antiquary, Philipp Baron von Stosch (ill.).[4] The twenty-six-year-old Stosch (1691-1727), emphasised his classical self-identification by his choice of simple inscription in Roman capitals on the reverse, 'MORIBVS ANTIQVIS'. He returned to Rome in 1722 on a dangerous diplomatic mission on behalf of England, and so was far from unknown in this country. It may be no coincidence that this was the very year when Stukeley sat to Le Marchand for his similar portrait in ivory. Some connection at least seems to be indicated by the introduction into the picture of Stukeley's own sketch for a medallion of Newton, made perhaps soon after Newton had refused to let Kneller draw his profile in 1720.

There is a bronze medal showing Stukeley's likeness done by Gaab in 1765 which seems to derive from Le Marchand's ivory. On the reverse of this medal is the inscription, 'aet. 54' (implying that the image was made in 1741), as well as a relief of Stonehenge, the study and publication of which is Stukeley's chief claim to fame, among many other accomplishments. It is interesting to note how in this case, as in those of Guy, Locke, Newton and Wren, Le Marchand was the influential precursor of later, hitherto better-known, portraitists of the 'British Worthies' in the mid-eighteenth century.

1 *Surtees Society*, 1882, p.131, n.26
2 *Surtees Society*, 73, 1882, pp.130-1: 'I left London to reside at Grantham, June, 1726. In two years' time I lost an incredible number of my most intimate friends there: Sir Isaac Newton; Ld. Winchester; Mr. Humphrey Wanley; my Ld Oxfords librarian; Charles Christian the famous cutter of intaglia's, &c; Mr. John Talman, the famous drawer and painter Monsr. Cheron; the famous cutter in ivory, Monsr. Marchand, who cut my profile; . . .'
3 Westfall, 1980, pp.849-51
4 Staatliche Museen, Berlin, Skulpturengalerie [744]: Theuerkauff, 1986, pp.241-8, no.66

54

Sir Godfrey Kneller Bt, *The Reverend William Stukeley MD*, pen, ink and wash, National Portrait Gallery, London (4266).

G. B. Pozzo, *Philipp Baron von Stosch*, ivory, Staatliche Museen Preussischer Kulturbesitz, Berlin (744).

Huguenots, City Businessmen and Artists

Le Marchand found his feet in London thanks to his Huguenot connections, some of whom were prominent businessmen in the City, or fellow-artists working in precious metals (like Michael Garnault, a jeweller), or wax (like Mathieu Gosset who signed the Oath Roll of Naturalization on the same day) or in clock-making (like Gamaliel Voyce), and their identities provide fascinating insights into the daily life of the metropolis at that period.

55★
Anne Dacier (1654-1720) Date unknown
Portrait medallion; profile to the left
12 (4¾)
The British Museum, London, No.462
Condition: good

PROV: Given by A.W. Franks Esq, 1879

LIT: Dalton, 1909, p.152, no.462; Reilly and Savage, 1973, p.117; Avery, 1984, p.116, pl.xviii(c)

Other example: plaster mould, Wedgwood Museum, Barlaston (No.341A); inscr. on edge: 'Mad. Daisier (No.341A) Scu dec'd', and on back of exterior 'Dacier'

Born Anne Lefèbre, she married the Huguenot scholar André Dacier, but like her husband embraced Catholicism upon the Revocation of the Edict of Nantes. Her works include many translations from classics such as the *Iliad* and *Odyssey*.

56★
Anonymous Man, possibly André Dacier Date unknown
Portrait medallion; profile to the right
12.75 × 10.2 (5 × 4)
HM The Queen, Windsor Castle
Condition: excellent
Inscr: (on the ground below the truncation) D.L.M.

PROV: Purchase by HM Queen Mary (£7/10/0); Presented to the Royal Library in 1935

LIT: Reilly and Savage, 1973, p.67, fig.(a)

Other example: plaster mould, Wedgwood Museum, Barlaston (No.281)

The sitter has been, probably incorrectly, identified as the French critic, Nicolas Boileau-Despréaux (1636-1711), because the name of Boileau is inscribed on the back of the mould at Barlaston (ill.). Reilly and Savage were quite rightly dubious of the identification, as the features are unlike those on medals by J. Dassier and Pesez (see Reilly and Savage, 1973, p.67, fig.b). It has also been wrongly suggested that the identity of the sitter may be that of 'Handel, in middle life'. Since the present profile bears little resemblance to those of either of these men, the identifications may safely be disregarded.

A clue to its correct identity may be inferred from the fact that a mould of it is paired in the Wedgwood Museum with that of Mrs Dacier (Cat.55), and listed accordingly in its Catalogue of 1773 (see Reilly and Savage, 1973). The dimensions of the respective ivory medallions are

56

After Le Marchand, *André Dacier (?)*, plaster mould, Wedgwood Museum, Barlaston.

55

approximately the same and so this gentleman may be her husband, André, a Huguenot scholar. Both embraced Catholicism in 1685 after the Revocation of the Edict of Nantes.

57*
Michael Garnault of Châtellerault (1669-1746) 1700-20
Portrait medallion; profile to the right
14.4 × 11.5 (5⅝ × 4½)
Collection of Lord Thomson of Fleet, Toronto
Condition: good
Inscr: (on the ground below the truncation of the shoulder) D.L.M.

PROV: H. Fernandes; Christie's, 13 December 1976, lot 109

EXH: Museum of London, 1985, no.309

LIT: H. Wagner, 'Notes to the pedigree of Garnault', *Proceedings of the Huguenot Society London*, XI, 1915-17, pp.149-51; Avery, 1984, pp.113, 115, 116, pl.XVIII (b)

Michael Garnault of Châtellerault, a Huguenot, was naturalised in 1703/4, and in 1727 (a year after Le Marchand's death) appeared as of St Peter's le Poor, a jeweller, Citizen and Loriner. He purchased Bowling Green House, Bull's Cross, Enfield, in 1724 and died 9 July 1746 without offspring, being buried in Enfield parish church.[1] Interestingly, he left legacies of £100 each to James Louis Berchère (1670-1753), a jeweller like himself, a banker and one of the original Directors of the French Hospital, as well as to the latter's son-in-law (who was also a jeweller) Louis Baril (1692-1761). Michael's sister Marie married James Dargent, almost certainly a member of the family of Parisian gold- and silversmiths, who had suffered under the Revocation.

Le Marchand shows Garnault at the height of his career wearing a luxuriant periwig, with his attire casually unbuttoned and a cloak thrown about his shoulders – a standard device for disguising the truncation of a bust: the carver's initials are tucked almost out of sight under the overhanging cloak.

'Michael Garnault's name has recently been discovered on an inventory of plate and jewels dated October 3rd, 1711 for the 2nd Duke of Bedford. The inventory is also signed by Francis Child and suggests that Garnault may have had connections with that Banking House. His brother Aimé Garnault (1717-82), became Treasurer of the New River Company.'[2]

1 Robinson, *History of Enfield*, London, 1882, I, pp.58-9; II, pp.269-70
2 Museum of London, 1985, p.210, no.309

58* (Plate 2)
Francis Sambrooke (b.1662) 1704
Bust
20 (7½)
Collection of Lord Thomson of Fleet, Toronto
Condition: good
Inscr: (on the reverse) Le Marchand fac. 1704 / Mr. Fran. Sambrooke Aetat Suae 42.

PROV: Sotheby's, 14 July 1977, lot 302 ('Property of a Lady'); Sotheby's, New York, 27 November 1981, lot 29 (unsold)

Francis Sambrooke, son and heir of Francis Sambrooke of The Close, Salisbury, Wiltshire, was admitted to the Middle Temple on 5 December 1682. He was the father of Frances Sambrooke who married John Russell (1697-1762), an ancestor of the owner previous to the vendor at Sotheby's.

The Sambrooke family were City merchants and Turkey traders, the most well known member of which was Sir Jeremiah Sambrooke, a contemporary of the present sitter who was knighted in 1681 on board the Earl of Berkeley's ship. (See Cat.27, the Countess of Berkeley)

57

58

Jeremiah was elected a Governor of St Thomas's Hospital in 1715, and was a trustee of Thomas Guy's will of 1725. This points to a relationship with several others of the sculptor's patrons.

This is one of the most impressively characterised and brilliantly carved of Le Marchand's busts.

59*
Gamaliel Voyce (1672-1712, or after) 1712
Portrait medallion; profile to the right
10.5 (4⅛)
The Victoria & Albert Museum, London, A.18-1936
Condition: cracked and slightly discoloured
Inscr: (on the ground below the truncation) D.L.M.F.; (on the reverse) Gamll. Voyce/ 1712/ Natus/ Decm 10/ 1672

PROV: Messrs Leitch and Kerin (£22 10s the pair)

LIT: Victoria & Albert Museum, *Review*, 1936, p.3

Other example: paired with Cat.60

Gamaliel Voyce probably belonged to a family of clockmakers: a Richard and Gamaliel Voyce are recorded as having been apprenticed as clockmakers in London, the latter in 1687 (F. J. Britten, *Old Clocks and Watches and their makers*, London, 6th ed., 1932, p.853). This would fit with the present man, who – having been born late in 1672 – would have been fourteen or fifteen in 1687, a normal age for entering an apprenticeship. Gamaliel could have been one of the St Martin's Lane clique and might possibly have been a naturalised Frenchman, originally by the name Voyez.

He was undoubtedly related in some way to Mary Voyce, and she was old enough to have been his mother (Cat.60).

A Jean Voyez carved later in the century a plaque showing *Prometheus Bound* (Holbourne of Menstrie Museum, Bath; Maskell, 1905, pp.384-5), and so it is possible that the Voyez were also *ivoiriers*, like David Le Marchand.

60*
Mary Voyce (1651-1729) *c*.1712 (?)
Portrait medallion; profile to the right
12 (4⅝)
The Victoria & Albert Museum, London A.19-1936
Condition: somewhat discoloured
Inscr: (on the ground below the truncation of the shoulder) D.L.M.; (on the reverse) natus 24 Augt/ 1651/ Mary Voyce/ Died ye 31 Augt/ Aged/ 78/ 1729

PROV: Messrs Leitch and Kerin (£22 10s the pair)

LIT: Victoria & Albert Museum, *Review*, 1936, p.3

Other example: paired with Cat.59

Mary Voyce was undoubtedly related in some way to Gamaliel Voyce (Cat.59) and, given their respective dates of birth, could have been his mother, as she would have been twenty-one in the year of his birth.

The date of her death, 1729, must have been inscribed by a hand other than Le Marchand's, for by then he had been dead himself for three years.

The portrait of this buxom, middle-aged lady may have been carved at the same date as Gamaliel's in 1712, when he was forty and she was sixty-one years old. Both look considerably younger than their inscribed dates of birth and the date of execution on Gamaliel's medallion state. Either they were exceptionally well-preserved, or David chose to flatter them by deducting some years from their countenances.

59

60

Le Marchand, the Raper Family and the Early Bank of England

The carver enjoyed a close relationship with one particular, powerful, merchant family, the Rapers. Most unusually his portrait was painted by Highmore along with those of the family. Three of the menfolk, Mathew I (1653-1713), a London silk merchant, and his two sons, Mathew II (1675-1748) and Moses (1679-1748), also a silkman and President of Guy's Hospital, were in succession Directors of the Bank of England.

This suggests that they had Whig and Huguenot sympathies, which may explain how they came across Le Marchand. He carved their profiles, together with Mrs Raper's, in ivory, as is now known only through plaster moulds taken from them, for possible use in the Wedgwood ceramic manufactory.

A third generation of the Rapers, Mathew III, was portrayed from life in 1720, at the age of fifteen, standing in the family library. Later in life he was to give the family bust of Sir Isaac Newton, carved by Le Marchand in 1716, to the nascent British Museum, along with a small profile medallion of Sir Christopher Wren.

Several of Le Marchand's sitters were early Directors of the Bank of England, founded in 1694. Among them was probably Sir John Houblon (1632-1712), first Governor, whose portrait graces the current £50 note; while another Director, Sir Humphry Morice, may have been the source of the ivory tusks used by the carver, for he was a merchant trading with West Africa.

61 (Illustrated on page 1)
Self-portrait(?) c.1710
Portrait medallion; profile to the left
11.5 × 9 ($4\frac{5}{8} \times 3\frac{3}{8}$)
Private Collection
Condition: perfect

PROV: 'Mr. T. West' (possibly James West of Alscot Park, Warwickshire); Christie's, 1969

LIT: Vertue, IV, p.61; Avery, 1984, p.114, pl.XVII (b)

In Vertue's *Notebooks* he mentions, 'D. L. Marchand Carver in Ivory, a profil in Ivory in a small oval frame. D.L.M. his own picture looking towards the left side. In posses Mr. T. West.' The indication that the sculptor was shown in profile to the left is a valuable clue, for there are only two Le Marchand medallions apart from the present one with a male sitter facing left, King James II (Cat.14) and one known only from a cast in wax at Wedgwood (Cat.89). Only in this one, are the features congruent – to say the least – with those in the portrait by Highmore, which shows Le Marchand as a rather bluff-looking man, proudly displaying his ivory bust of Newton (see Cat.68; front cover and detail: ill.p.21).

The identity of the owner named by Vertue is not known, if the initial of the christian name has been transcribed correctly. If, however, the letter is a crossed 'J' and not a 'T', it could stand for James West of Alscot Park, Warwickshire, a prominent antiquarian and collector, in whose posthumous sales by Langford and Son in 1772-3 there appeared a small ivory bust of Newton that – in the absence of other candidates for its authorship – is almost certainly one by Le Marchand (Cat.47).

62
Mathew Raper II (1675-1748) c.1720
Portrait medallion; profile to the right
c.11 ($4\frac{3}{4}$)
Lost
Inscr: (below the truncation) D.L.M.

PROV: Raper family

LIT: Avery, 1984, p.115; Avery, 1985, p.1564, fig.4

Other examples: see Cats 62a, 62b, 62c

The existence of this medallion may be inferred from moulds taken from it by Wedgwood and, probably, by James Tassie, from which casts in ceramic (modern) and glass-paste (c.1770) respectively, have been made. To save confusion, these are catalogued separately below. This medallion forms a pair with one of his wife, Mary Elizabeth (née Billers) also by Le Marchand, and also lost, but known through the mould (Cat.63a).

These moulds in plaster of Paris at Wedgwood are inscribed on the outside in pencil 'Mr. and Mrs. Raper', and the images are typical of Le Marchand, showing his inimitable handling of drapery and hair. This is corroborated by the name 'Mathew Raper Esqre. Senior' inscribed in ink on the paper backing to the frame of the glass-paste medallion (Cat.62a).

Son of Mathew Raper I (1653-1713), merchant of London and a Director of the Bank of England (1712-13), by his first wife, Elizabeth, Mathew II was born in 1675, four years before his brother Moses (Cat.64). Mathew II married in 1705 Mary Elizabeth, daughter of another London merchant, William Billers, Haberdasher. She must have promptly borne him a son, whom they named Mathew, the third of that name, for on the portrait dated 1720 that they presumably commissioned from Le Marchand he is described as in his fifteenth year. Mathew II was a silkman, a Member of the Dissenting Deputies Committee and a Director of the Bank of England more or less continuously between his first election in 1730 and his death on 18 June 1748. The couple lived at Wendover Dean in Buckinghamshire, but later moved to Thorley, where there is a monument to them.

Mathew II was, like his brother Moses, a Trustee of Guy's Hospital. He, or Moses, may have commissioned – or acquired – the Le Marchand busts of Newton (Cat.68) and Locke (Cat.69) as a pair.

62a⋆
After Le Marchand, attributed to James Tassie
Mathew Raper II (1665-1748) c.1770
Glass-paste medallion; profile to the right
11 ($4\frac{3}{4}$)
The Victoria & Albert Museum, London, C.214-1987
Condition: restored break below truncation

Inscr: (below the truncation) D.L.M.
A paper backing is inscribed in an old hand in ink 'Mathew Raper Esqre. Senior'

PROV: Christie's Silver Sale, 11 July 1985, lot 10

LIT: Reilly and Savage, 1973, p.286; Avery, 1985, p.1564

Other examples: see Cats 62, 62b

James Tassie was closely associated with Wedgwood, and D. Gray's catalogue of the work of James and William Tassie (London, 1984) lists portraits of both William Raper and his wife (both of which were included in the same lot at Christie's), although no mention is made of the medallion of Mathew Raper. However, the use of glass-paste and the fact that all three medallions appeared together suggest that Tassie was the author of the present medallion.

The initials of David Le Marchand on this medallion support Reilly's and Savage's suggestion that the Wedgwood portrait of Mathew Raper II is after Le Marchand (Cat.62b). Mathew Raper II, a silkman and later a Director of the Bank of England, commissioned – or acquired – the Le Marchand busts of Locke (Cat.69) and Newton (Cat.68) as a pair. He must also have commissioned from Le Marchand in 1720 a full-length portrait of his son, Mathew III (Cat.64).

62b★
After lost Le Marchand ivory
Mathew Raper II (1665-1748) 1972
Modern ceramic medallion
$c.11 \left(4\frac{3}{4}\right)$
Wedgwood Museum, Barlaston

LIT: Reilly and Savage, 1973, p.286; Avery, 1984, p.115; Avery, 1985, p.1564, fig.4

Other examples: see Cats 62, 62a

The image is cast from old moulds from the Wedgwood Factory which are labelled on the outside in pencil 'Mr. and Mrs. Raper'. The moulds were presumably taken from an original wax model or ivory medallion by Le Marchand.

There is a record of Wedgwood & Co paying 6d to James Hoskins in 1773-4 for two moulds 'from Ivery' [sic], among a number of others from diverse sources. The moulds were taken from the ivory originals with a view to reproducing them in ceramic, though no old examples are known, and perhaps none was manufactured.

63★
Mrs Mary Elizabeth Raper, née Billers (1683-1760) c.1720
Portrait medallion; profile to the left
$10.5 \left(4\frac{1}{8}\right)$
Lost

PROV: Raper family

LIT: Reilly and Savage, 1973, p.286

Other examples: see Cats 63a, 63b

For discussion, see Cats 62, 62b

This was a pair to Le Marchand's medallion of Mathew Raper II, and is known only from an old mould and a fragmentary wax cast (No.2422) inscribed on the reverse 'Mrs. Raper', in the Wedgwood Museum, Barlaston.

Daughter of William Billers, Haberdasher of London, Mary Elizabeth married Mathew Raper II in 1705, while her younger sister Martha married in 1707 his younger brother Moses. She bore Mathew Raper III quite promptly, for he was in his fifteenth year in 1720, according to the inscription on the reverse of his portrait plaque (Cat.64).

62a

62b

63b

63a
After Le Marchand
Mrs Mary Elizabeth Raper, née Billers (1683-1760) *c*.1770
Wax portrait medallion; profile to the left
10.5 (4⅛)
Wedgwood Museum, Barlaston (No.2422)
Condition: fragmentary
Inscr: (on the reverse) 'Mrs. Raper'

PROV: Old factory site

LIT: Reilly and Savage, 1973, p.286

Other examples: see Cats 63, 63b

For discussion, see Cats 62, 62b

63b★
After Le Marchand
Mrs Mary Elizabeth Raper, née Billers (1683-1760) 1972
Modern ceramic portrait medallion; profile to the left
10.5 (4⅛)
Wedgwood Museum, Barlaston

PROV: Cast from old mould

LIT: Reilly and Savage, 1973, p.286

Other examples: see Cats 63, 63a

For discussion, see Cats 62, 62b

64★ (Plate 4)
Mathew Raper III FRS (1704-1778) 1720
Rectangular portrait relief; full-length
20.16 × 15.71 (7¹⁵⁄₁₆ × 6³⁄₁₆)
The Victoria & Albert Museum, London, A.10-1959
Condition: cracked; and finger missing from sitter's right hand
Inscr: (on the reverse) Eff. Mathei RAPER juni/ AEtat. suae 15 An./ad Viv. Scul. D.L.M. 1720

PROV: C. L. Grindwater, 9 Elgin Avenue, London W9; Acquired by the Victoria & Albert Museum, 1959

EXH: Museum of London, 1985, no.308

LIT: Hodgkinson, 1965, pp.29-32, fig.2; Whinney, 1971, p.26, no.1; Kerslake, 1972, pp.25-9; Avery, 1984, pp.113-18, fig.9; Avery, 1985, p.1564, fig.6

Mathew Raper III was the son of Mathew Raper II, a silk merchant of Wendover Dean, Buckinghamshire, who became a Director of the Bank of England in 1738 (Cat.62). This remarkable relief shows the young Mathew full-length, at the age of fifteen, standing in a library and demonstrating a proposition in geometry. The exceptional format and casually studious pose of the Raper heir were derived from French Court portraiture of intellectuals under Louis XIV, with which David would have been familiar from his background in Dieppe, in order to flatter both father and son.

As Hodgkinson wrote in 1965: 'there is no parallel in Le Marchand's

work for the legs swathed in a windswept gown, the perspective effect of the floorboards, the bookcase and the table. These features seem to be derived from two different conventions. The formal pose of the feet and the irrationally billowing drapery suggest the court portraiture of Rigaud, which was probably known to Le Marchand through the engravings of Pierre Drevet. A similar bookcase with a volume inclined across a gap often appears in the background of Rigaud portraits; an example is that of the poet Boileau-Despréaux, engraved by Drevet in 1706 [ill.p.89]. The bare floor and the realistically rendered tripod table, on the other hand, recall the bourgeois portraits and conversation pieces which originated in the Netherlands; they had been fashionable for some years in France, and were to gain favour rapidly in England in the course of the 1720's. No other sculptor is known to have carved a portrait of this kind.'

Indeed, there is a distinct similarity in the pose and 'flattened', inaccurate perspective of the setting that recalls contemporary French popular engravings of the period, for instance, the frontispiece of *Le Parfumeur François*, 3rd ed., Amsterdam, 1696. First published in 1693, this compendium deals not only with perfumes, but also with scenting tobacco, and the latter might have brought it to the notice of an ivory carver, some of whose traditional work in relief was for the ornamental outsides of tobacco rasps and snuff-boxes.

The reverse of this plaque is fascinating on account of the inscription scrawled across it as if with a quill pen, though the carver actually had to translate his handwriting with a burin, to engrave it deep into the surface of the ivory. The information that this inscription conveys has been discussed, but the epigraphy too is of interest.

The strongly looped D and sinuous L of his own initials correspond well with those of his signature as a witness at a baptism in May 1705 (ill.p.18) and on the Oath Roll of Naturalization in 1709 (ill.p.18). The scratchy M, with its splaying 'legs', is recognisable in his other signature of 3 March 1706 (ill.p.18), where, however, he omitted the 'Le' from his name and wrote the initial D with a grand carelessness, when compared to the conscientiously neat hands of the other signatories.

65
Moses Raper (?) (1679-1748) 1716-20
Portrait medallion; profile to the right
10.5 × 8.5 (4⅛ × 3⅜)
Lost

LIT: Kerslake, 1972, pp.27-8, pl.7; Reilly and Savage, 1973, p.348 (b)

Other examples: see Cats 65a, 65b

The existence of this medallion may be inferred from an old mould preserved in the Wedgwood Museum, Barlaston (Cat.65a), which is inscribed on the exterior '[Mr. Moses (?)] Raper'. While the christian name is hard to decipher, the surname is quite clear, and the profile matches well the painted three-quarter face portrait by Highmore (ill.p.20). It appears that Wedgwood acquired among his wax casts of works by Le Marchand a clutch of those which depicted members of the Raper family, his favourite patrons.

As Kerslake wrote in 1972: 'In the history of a family it is usually the chief protagonists of the family fortune who are commemorated by portraits; in the Raper family one would rather expect the successive owners of Thorley to be so commemorated. The man who brought Thorley to the family was Moses Raper (1679-1748), a silkman of London who purchased it in 1714 from William, son of John Billers, citizen and haberdasher of London. Moses became a Director of the Bank of England in 1716 and remained so until 1742, was a governor of St Thomas' Hospital and of Guy's Hospital, where he presented an operating theatre in 1739, and was a trustee of Guy's residuary estate. Thomas Guy, who died in 1724, was also portrayed by Le Marchand and the relief is in the Victoria and Albert. The portrait said to be of "Beau" Raper would fit Moses very well about the time he purchased Thorley and became a director of the Bank.'

Son of Mathew Raper I, married in 1707 Martha Billers, sister of Mary Elizabeth (Cat.63), who had married his elder brother Mathew II two years earlier. It was from his father-in-law that Moses purchased Thorley in 1714. Moses was childless and his wife predeceased him on 18 March 1725. He died on 30 March 1748 and is buried at Thorley, Hertfordshire, where there is a monument. His brother Mathew followed him to the grave ten weeks later.

65a*
After Le Marchand
Moses Raper (?) (1679-1748) 1972
Modern ceramic portrait medallion; profile to the right
10.5 × 8.5 ($4\frac{1}{8}$ × $3\frac{3}{8}$)
Wedgwood Museum, Barlaston

PROV: Cast from old mould

LIT: Kerslake, 1972, pp.27-8, p.17; Reilly and Savage, 1973, p.348 (b)

Other example: see Cat.65

Reilly and Savage correctly suggest that the style of this relief is that of Le Marchand.

66*
The Miracle of Christ healing the Man with the Withered Hand
*c.*1720
Ivory narrative relief
*c.*13.4 × 20.75 ($5\frac{1}{4}$ × $8\frac{1}{8}$)
The National Museum of Wales, Cardiff
Condition: good
Inscr: (on the ground at bottom left) D.L.M./in. &/ Sc.

PROV: Given by F. E. Andrews (1932)

EXH: Museum of London, 1985, no.303

LIT: Avery, 1984, pp.113-18; Theuerkauff, 1984, p.92, n.11

This is the only surviving religious narrative relief definitely by David, who proclaimed his invention as well as execution in his signature, though a signed one showing the *Adoration of the Magi* was recorded in the hands of an antique dealer in Paris towards the beginning of this century.[1]

Other reliefs of *Charity* (Cat.94) and of *Apollo and the Muses on Mount Parnassus* (Cat.98) are attributed to him. In view of his descent from a family of painters active in Dieppe, it is surprising that not more narrative reliefs are known, for they were a staple product of many a continental carver of the period, men such as Ignaz Elhafen or Van Opstal. Possibly the explanation is to be found in the Protestantism of his adopted country, which meant that Christian imagery was suspected of being 'Popish'. Even so, classical subjects might have appealed to connoisseurs in the days of the early Grand Tour, if one thinks of the four fine bronze reliefs of *The Seasons* by Soldani that were imported into England by the young Lord Burlington as early as 1714.[2] Possibly David's penchant for portraiture was therefore an indication not just of his clients' orders, but a personal choice, based perhaps on a recognition of the rather hazardous grasp of proportion and movement evinced in such narratives and figurines as he did carve. He certainly had not

Drevet, after Hyacinthe Rigaud, *Nicolas Boileau-Despréaux*, engraving, Victoria & Albert Museum, London.

65a

enjoyed the privilege of a study journey to Italy, and probably lacked formal training too, other than from his father, owing to the fraught circumstances of his youth, after the Revocation of the Edict of Nantes in 1685 (see p.13).

The present relief bravely sets out to dramatise the spiritual conflict between Christ and a critical rabbi by making them face each other in profile across the shallow, sloping stage, flanking the man with the withered arm who stands at the very centre of the composition. The eye focuses on his sadly bent hand, which contrasts forlornly with the wagging finger of the rabbi and Christ's almost Leonardesque gesture upwards with his index finger. The trio are equidistantly spaced in front of pilasters indicating an architectural setting. The attendant figures in the middle and rear grounds are not entirely satisfactory, for the looping folds of their drapery that Le Marchand used to bind the composition together are actually so exaggerated as to be distracting.

The reason for interpolating this panel among the portraits of, and busts belonging to, the Rapers, is that the involvement of Moses Raper with Guy's Hospital suggests him as a possible source for such a commission. One knows that Guy himself was not concerned with art, and yet one can imagine a rich and enthusiastic supporter who was so interested, one such as Moses, wanting to honour Guy's charitable work by likening it to that of Christ. Indeed on the flanks of the pedestal that supports Scheemakers' posthumous bronze statue of Mr Guy in the forecourt of his hospital, are set two bronze reliefs for this very reason: *The Good Samaritan* and *Christ healing the Palsied Man.* These date from well after Guy's and indeed Le Marchand's deaths in the mid-1720s, but serve to point to a possible rationale for the carver to have made an exception to his rule of avoiding narrative sculpture.

If this hypothesis has any validity, it would point to a date early in the 1720s, after Guy had become inordinately rich from his profits in the South Sea Company and his decision to found his hospital, and yet before the carver became too infirm before his own death in 1726. Its similarities with the setting, treatment of drapery and general style of the plaque depicting Mathew Raper III in 1720 serve to corroborate this dating.

1 Lami, 1906, p.317
2 C. Avery, 'Soldani's bronze reliefs of *Summer* and *Autumn*: new documentation and observations on their date and patronage', *The Register of the Spencer Art Museum*, University of Kansas, Lawrence, Kansas, 1995/6 (in the press)

67*
Sir Christopher Wren (1632-1723) 1723 (?)
Portrait medallion; profile to the right
10.2 (4)
The British Museum, London, No.457
Condition: good
Inscr: (on the ground below the truncation) D.L.M.; (on the reverse) CHRISTOPH WREN EQ. AV.

PROV: Given by Mathew Raper III FRS, 1765

LIT: Dalton, 1909, no.457, p.152; Longhurst, 1926, p.60; National Portrait Gallery, *Annual Report of the Trustees 1966-67*, HMSO, 1967, p.33; Avery, 1984, pp.113, 114; Avery, 1985, p.1564

Other examples: Cat.48; plaster mould, Wedgwood Museum, Barlaston (No.309A): inscribed on either side of exterior 'Sir Christopher Wren'

This medallion, together with the bust of Newton (Cat.68), was presented to the nascent British Museum in 1765 by Mathew Raper III (Cat.64). It has been suggested by the National Portrait Gallery that

66

67

this portrait, being less vivid than their example, may have been made at second hand, rather than from life. Indeed, the rather crude inscription on the verso is not dissimilar from that on the medallion of Stukeley carved in 1722 (Cat.54). This might therefore date from the following year, 1723, when Wren himself died, and David may have been ailing.

68* (Back cover image)
Sir Isaac Newton PRS (1642-1727) 1718
Bust
24 (9¾)
The British Museum, London, No.455
Condition: discoloured
Inscr: (on back of stand) ISAACUS NEWTON / EQ: AVRA / An: 1718 / Le Marchand / Sc. ad vi.

PROV: Mathew Raper Esq FRS, 1765

LIT: Dussieux, 1876, p.273; Maze-Sencier, 1885, p.639; Lami, 1906, p.317; Dalton, 1909, p.151, no.455, pl.CVIII; Vertue, II, p.69; Kerslake, 1972, p.26, figs 3, 4, 5; Westfall, 1980, pp.752, 854; Avery, 1984, p.114, pl.XVII (c); Avery, 1985, p.1563, pl.3; Gjertsen, 1986, p.444, *Busts*, no.2; Neil McGregor, 'Choice', in *British Museum Magazine*, Winter, 1994, no.20, p.32

Other examples: see Cats 47, 69b, 69d

This bust is wrongly identified by Dalton (1909) with an item in the sale of the collection of Dr Mead in 1755, but that was in fact a relief (Cat.44). It appears to be the one held by the subject of Highmore's portrait, which is believed to represent Le Marchand himself (see front cover and detail: ill.p.21). It was therefore probably commissioned by the Rapers, his great patrons, for it was presented to the British Museum (together with an oval medallion depicting Sir Christopher Wren) in 1765 by Mathew Raper III. Its inscription, giving the information that it was carved from life in 1718, corresponds closely with that shown in the painting, though Highmore has turned it towards the spectator for better legibility. The bust was presumably commissioned by either Mathew Raper II, the donor's father, or Moses, his uncle, unless it is the one that Sir Isaac himself had commissioned, which after his death was recorded as having cost him one hundred guineas. This the Rapers might have acquired, before Mathew III gave it to the British Museum.

69* (Plate 11)
John Locke (1632-1704) *c.*1718(?)
Bust
21.5 (8½)
Lost
Condition: cracked
Inscr: (on the reverse of the stand) Effi. IOHAis Locke/Aetat: 65/ D.L.M.Sc.; (in ink inside the right shoulder) Raper

PROV: Raper family; [?Alfred Morrison]; Mrs Michael Wright, 3 Barton Street, London SW1 (1936)

EXH: [?] Burlington Fine Arts Club, London, 1879, no.70

LIT: Burlington Fine Arts Club, *Catalogue of Bronzes and Ivories of European Origin, exhibited in 1879*, London, 1879, no.70; 'Bust of Locke, H. 8 in. – Mr Alfred Morrison'; Avery, 1984, p.114, pl.XVII (d); Avery, 1985, p.1562, pls 1, 2

After Sir Godfrey Kneller Bt, *John Locke*, National Portrait Gallery, London (550).

68

69

Other examples: see Cats 69a, 69c

This bust was left for study at the Victoria & Albert Museum in 1936 and is now known only from photographs taken at the time and a facsimile of the signature and inscription made by Margaret Longhurst. At first sight, an approximate date of the portrait can be calculated from the inscribed age of the sitter: 1697. However, this is very early in Le Marchand's career, when he was probably still in Edinburgh. Locke sat for Kneller in the same year, and as Le Marchand does not state that he executed this portrait from life, the Latin inscription may rather mean, 'the likeness of John Locke at 65 years old'. If that were the case, it could have been carved at any subsequent date, using Kneller's three-quarter face image (ill.p.91), and other, later portraits too, as a guide. It may indeed have been made after Locke's death in 1704. Its similarity in size and drapery to the bust of Newton of 1718 and the fact that the Rapers once owned both, point to a date around then.

The two images were certainly treated as a pair quite early on, for they were reproduced as such twice, though with a decreasing degree of veracity as regards the originals. In the presumably earlier pair (Cats 69a, 69b) the portraits are respectably close, though less naturalistic and distinctly stylised. They have classically blank eyes, which gives them a funereal look, but this is perhaps not intended, for while Locke had died in 1704, Newton survived until 1727, a year after Le Marchand's death, and so if this pair *is* by him, it must antedate that event. However, neither is signed or identified in any way. This is supicious, in view of the full data inscribed on the prime versions, unless, as is not impossible, one presumes that they were brought forward this far by David, and that he was prevented from applying the finishing touches, such as the pupils of the eyes and signature, perhaps overtaken by what was to prove his final illness early in 1726.

What seems to be the second – or at least the less good – pair (Cats 69c, 69d) confusingly does have the names of the subjects inscribed on the supports behind in a curious mixture of capital and lower-case letters with (barely necessary) abbreviations, in an approximation of Le Marchand's careless hand, as it appears on other ivories. However, the extraordinary and suspicious feature of this pair is that, while the Locke resembles fairly well David's lost bust that once belonged to the Rapers, the Newton has lost his distinctly smoother, harder face, so that his features and even his hair resemble much more closely those of the Locke with which it is paired. This does suggest the work of a copyist – perhaps one of the apprentices whom the carver had been obliged to train in Edinburgh and who might have followed him to London subsequently.

69a
Perhaps by Le Marchand
John Locke (1632-1704) 1720-5
Bust
19.75 (7¾)
Collection of Lord Thomson of Fleet, Toronto
Condition: cracked and breaks in forelock

PROV: Mrs Kavan (sold Sotheby's, 26 March 1965, lot 7)

Other examples: see Cats 69, 69c

The bust is paired with one of Newton (Cat.69b). As in the case of its pair, the patterns of the drapery and hair differ from those of the prime version.

For discussion, see Cat.69

69b
Perhaps by Le Marchand
Sir Isaac Newton PRS (1642-1727) 1720-5
Bust
19 (7½)
Collection of Lord Thomson of Fleet, Toronto
Condition: cracked and discoloured

PROV: Mrs Kavan (sold Sotheby's, 26 March 1965, lot 7)

Other examples: see Cats 47, 68, 69d

The bust is paired with one of Locke (Cat.69a). As in the case of its pair, the patterns of the drapery and hair differ from those of the prime version.

For discussion, see Cat.69

69a

69c

After Le Marchand

John Locke (1632-1704) 1725-50

Bust

20 $(7\frac{15}{16})$

Collection of Lord Thomson of Fleet, Toronto

Condition: good

Inscr: (on the support at the back) ioHaN Locke

PROV: Purchased from Alfred Speelman, 1953

Other examples: see Cats 69, 69a

The bust is paired with one of Newton (Cat.69d). Here, the patterns of the drapery and hair are similar to those of the prime version.

For discussion, see Cat.69

69d

After Le Marchand

Sir Isaac Newton PRS (1642-1727) 1725-50

Bust

20 $(7\frac{7}{8})$

Collection of Lord Thomson of Fleet, Toronto

Condition: good

Inscr: (on the support at the back) ISAA. NEWTO. Eq. A.G.

PROV: Purchased from Alfred Speelman, 1953

Other examples: see Cats 47, 68, 69b

The bust is paired with one of Locke (Cat.69c), whose patterns of drapery and hair, as well as the features of the face, it begins to approximate.

For discussion, see Cat.69

70★ (Plate 8)

Sir John Houblon, Lord Mayor of London (1632-1712)? *c.*1710

Oval portrait medallion; full-frontal

21.3 × 16 $(8\frac{3}{8} \times 6\frac{1}{4})$

Fondation d'Art du Docteur Rau, Embrach, Switzerland

Condition: cracked and discoloured; repairs in ivory to either side.

Inscr: (on the ground below the truncation of the shoulder) D.L.M.fec.

PROV: G. Buckston Browne Esq, 80 Wimpole Street, London W1; Sotheby's, 27 April 1945, lot 62; Sotheby's, 14 December 1978, lot 232

EXH: BFAC, 1923, no.220, pl.LI; *Charles II Loan Exhibition*, London, 1932, no.131

LIT: Longhurst, 1926, p.59; F. Davis, 'Talking about Salerooms', in *Country Life*, 29 March 1979, pp.902-3; C. Theuerkauff, unpublished catalogue entry for the present owner

69b

69c

69d

Thanks to its relatively early recognition, as well as the fact of its exhibition in London in 1923, this is one of the more celebrated of David's reliefs. Its large size and the direct, unflinching gaze of the sitter engage a viewer's attention immediately, leading Longhurst, for instance, to write of it in her book of 1926, 'a magnificent portrait medallion on an unusually large scale'.

The natural wish to know the identity of the subject and to associate such a grand portrait with a notable name, led to a tentative comparison with Samuel Pepys, whose features are indeed not wholly dissimilar. The author of the entry in the catalogue of the exhibition in 1923, where it is described as Samuel Pepys, notes that it 'does not correspond very well with the absolutely authenticated medallion of Pepys by Cavalier and may represent some other personage of the period'. Le Marchand's portrait of Pepys in the British Museum might also have been adduced (Cat.40). John Kerslake of the National Portrait Gallery wrote to the present author in 1978, 'I don't believe it is Pepys, and as far as we are concerned it is an unknown man'. Sotheby's in their catalogue entry also dismissed the erroneous identification, as does Theuerkauff, who calls it, 'offensichtlich *nicht* Samuel Pepys', by comparison with the authentic three-quarter face portrait painted by John Closterman in the National Portrait Gallery.[1]

The question therefore remains, who might this determined-looking, middle-aged gentleman be? As with any such identification, in the absence of specific documentation, one relies on a combination of circumstantial evidence and a subjective judgment as to the likeness of the sitter in the ivory to that in other authenticated portraits of a given candidate. When looking into the connections of Le Marchand's favourite patrons, the Rapers, with the Bank of England, it appeared that their fellow Directors on the relatively small Court (twenty-six members in all) might also have commissioned portraits from him.

The present medallion closely resembles a mezzotint by R. Williams (ill.p.95) after Closterman's three-quarter length painting celebrating Sir John Houblon's term as Lord Mayor of London in 1696, coinciding in date with the arrival of Le Marchand in Edinburgh. Curiously enough, it is an image which anyone examining currently a 'new' fifty pound note will find staring him in the face, beside an engraving of Sir John's house in Threadneedle Street for – after the death of his widow in 1732 – it became the third, and indeed the present, site of the Bank.[2]

As Dr Tessa Murdoch has written:[3] 'The Houblons were a remarkable merchant family, a father and five sons, who were noted for their success, liberality and mutual affection. They traded with France, Portugal, Spain and the Mediterranean. Their father, James (1592-1682), was the son of a Huguenot refugee from Lille. He lived in Bearbinder Lane in a house which he rebuilt after the Fire. One of his sons, also James, was a particular friend of Samuel Pepys. Sir John, the third eldest son, knighted in 1689, was Lord Mayor 1695-6, and the first Governor of the Bank of England (1694-7). He was also an Admiralty Commissioner (1694-9) and Master of the Grocers' Company in 1696.'

It seems unlikely that Le Marchand was in a position to carve such a large and impressive portrait as early as Houblon's *annus mirabilis* of 1696, though its resemblance to Closterman's portrait is so close as to suggest that the carver may have used it to copy from: they share the wide-set, large, searching eyes with flesh overhanging the upper lids, marked indentations below the sinuses, flabby, sunken cheeks and wide

mouth with protruding fleshy lower lip, not to mention the pronounced lines running from the sides of the nose to just above the corners of the mouth, the indented chin and comfortable double-chin. Le Marchand released the pressure of the latter on the tight white stock depicted by Closterman, by allowing the shirt to be unbuttoned in fashionable undress.

Theuerkauff has noted the extreme difficulty of dating works by Le Marchand on stylistic grounds alone, but cautiously concluded that this relief dated from the first decade, possibly preceding the bust of Lord Somers (Cat.37), which is dated 1706. This proposed dating corresponds well with the data of Houblon's career, granted that Le Marchand was probably in London by the time that he carved it (*ie* probably post-1700) and that Houblon died in 1712.

However, despite the lively look of the sitter, in the absence of the inscription '*ad vivum*', the portrait may not be from life, and therefore need not date from within the subject's lifetime. Closterman's portrait was all that a competent carver such as David would have needed in order to raise from the two-dimensional original a respectable sculptural facsimile.

If it were not commissioned by Houblon himself, or his grieving widow (who survived him by twenty years), then perhaps one of his fellow Directors of the Bank might have done so after his death in 1712. The Rapers are possible candidates, for they were neighbours, in Hertfordshire, of the Houblons, who lived at Great Hallingbury. Mathew Raper I, was a Director of the Bank in 1712 until his death in July 1713, and, being a near contemporary of Sir John, might have wished to honour him with a portrait. Failing that, his son Moses, elected to the Court of the Bank of England in 1716, might have wished to do so and, as we have seen, he was probably Le Marchand's prime patron at this period. The medallion, if indeed it does represent Sir John Houblon, might then date from the second decade of the eighteenth century, rather than the first.

1 J. Piper, *Catalogue of Seventeenth Century Portraits in the National Portrait Gallery, London*, Cambridge, 1963, pp.269f., nos 210, 211
2 B. R. James, *The New £50 Note and Sir John Houblon*, Loughton, 1994
3 Museum of London, 1985, p.276, no.412

71* (Plate 1)

Sir Humphry Morice, Governor of the Bank of England (1679-1731)(?) 1716-20

Bust in deep relief, full-face, including the sitter's right hand
14 × 11 ($5\frac{1}{2}$ × $4\frac{1}{4}$)
Lord Thomson of Fleet, London
Condition: good
Inscr: (on reverse) D.L.M.F.

PROV: Spencer's of Retford, sale 29 April 1987, lot 154

This half-length portrait is unusual, though not unique, in Le Marchand's *oeuvre* in being cut out round the edge, perhaps to be laid down on to a background of coloured material – semi-precious stone, or velvet, for example – or even on mirror-glass, as is recorded in another similar case (see Cat.50).

The subject of this striking and unusual portrait was tentatively identified as Sir Isaac Newton at the time of its sale, though with some reservations. However, recent research into the Rapers' fellow Directors of the Bank of England has revealed that the portrait resembles strikingly a painted portrait in the Bank of England Museum by Sir Godfrey Kneller of Sir Humphry Morice (ill.), who was a Director between 1716 and 1731, and Governor (after Le Marchand's death) from 1727 to 1729.

The proportions of the face and features are virtually identical. Both portraits, albeit in divers media, convey a self-confident air, through the square set of the chin, with a central cleft, purposefully closed lips, with the flanking muscles taught, and a direct gaze. In the bust, the inclusion of a hand, gracefully fingering the edge of the cloak – in truly Bernini-esque fashion (compare, for example, his bust of Thomas Baker in the Victoria & Albert Museum) – adds to the impression of dignity and self-esteem. The treatment of this hand is similar to that of the delicately-fingered hands in David's portrait of Mathew Raper III (Cat.64).

Information kindly provided by Mr Keyworth, the Curator, reads as follows:

'Morice was a prosperous merchant with a reputation for business acumen and integrity but shortly after his death in November 1731 it was found that among debts of £150,000 were fictitious bills amounting to £29,000 which he had discounted with the Bank. After prolonged litigation with his widow, £12,000 was eventually recovered and the remainder written off under "profit and loss". One explanation that has been offered for Morice's financial embarrassment is that he subscribed large sums to the Whig cause in the hope of a future peerage and died before he could repay the unauthorised "loan".'

What is even more germane is the fact that Morice was involved in the slave trade (to which of course at the time little stigma would have applied), as well as in the complementary trade in ivory tusks from the same parts of the Guinea Coast in West Africa, as were several other European nations, including the Dutch, French, Portuguese and Germans.[1] It may be through him that the carver obtained much of his raw material, at least during the middle part of his career, when they were in contact, thanks to Morice sitting alongside Moses Raper on the Court of Directors of the Bank of England (p.25).

Members of two other families who patronised Le Marchand, the Nelthorpes (see Cat.77) and the Eyres (see Cats 73-5), also invested £2000 each in Morice's African Trade venture, for they were recommended to him by none other than Sir Robert Walpole, the first Prime Minister, in a letter from Houghton on 17 June 1720.[2]

This strengthens the hypothesis that Sir Humphry knew David's work and might have commissioned the present fine image.

1 Bank of England Archive, COU. No.B.367/3, unpublished, selective, typscript entitled: *The Morice Letters, 1701-1731: A collection of letters written by Humphry Morice, sometime Governor of the Bank of England*, ed. W. Marston Acres FRHS
2 See Cat.77, note 2, for transcription

R. Williams, after J. Closterman, *Sir John Houblon* (detail), mezzotint, Bank of England Museum, London.

Sir Godfrey Kneller Bt, *Sir Humphry Morice*, Bank of England, London.

Other Portrait Medallions and Busts, the 'Wedgwood Connection'

A number of David's other portraits are of people outside the circles mentioned above: two of the families represented, the Eyres and the Nelthorpes, were connected by family and business ties. Among the anonymous medallions, two of the most striking are those of a young man and an older lady from the Fitzwilliam Museum, Cambridge. Several others are recorded in wax casts preserved in the Wedgwood Museum, Barlaston. These formed part of the stock-in-trade of Wedgwood and Bentley, along with myriad portrait images by other artists, from various sources such as Isaac Gosset the wax-modeller, who was in stylistic terms Le Marchand's successor. James Tassie also reused at least one of Le Marchand's models later in the century, as part of his series of medallic portraits in glass paste (Cat.62a). They are of interest inasmuch as they record ivory originals that are long lost.

72*
The Rt Hon. Elizabeth, Lady Cathcart, née Malyn (c.1691-1789)
1712-22
Portrait medallion; profile to the left
10×9 ($3\frac{15}{16} \times 3\frac{9}{16}$)
The Royal Museum of Scotland, Edinburgh
Condition: good
Paper label on the reverse of the frame 'Lady Cathcart (1686(?)-1789) prototype of the imprisoned lady in Castle Rackrent, see Edw. Ford's "Tewin Water" 1876'

PROV: Private Collection; Christie's, 7 April 1981, lot 93

LIT: J. B. Paul (ed.), The Scots Peerage . . . , Edinburgh, II, 1905, p.52; see also Edward Ford, 'Tewin Water' or the Story of Lady Cathcart; being a supplement to the History of Enfield, Enfield, 1876; E. W. Brayley, Beauties of England and Wales, London, 1808, VII, Hertfordshire . . ., p.270; and Maria Edgeworth, Castle Rackrent, an Hibernian Tale. Taken from facts and manners of the Irish squires before the year 1782, London/Dublin, 1800

The style of this high-relief portrait is unmistakably that of Le Marchand, being similar, for instance, to that of Anne Dacier (Cat.55). The medallion is not unique in being unsigned: the artist tended to initial only one out of a pair of portraits of husband and wife.

The sitter's identity is based solely on a presumption that the information given on the paper label behind is correct.[1] The Rt Hon. Elizabeth, Dowager Lady Cathcart, died at Tewin Water, Hertfordshire, on 3 August 1789 and is buried in St Peter's Tewin, where some information is recorded on her tombstone. As Ford writes: 'the strange history of whose life can hardly be surpassed in the wildest inventions of fiction'.

Daughter of an eminent brewer of Southwark and Battersea by the name of Thomas Malyn Esq who lived at Enfield Chase, her beauty caught the eye of, among others, Sir Richard Steele (see Cat.53). She would probably also have known another of Le Marchand's patron's, Michael Garnault, for he lived nearby (see Cat.57).

Elizabeth first married James Fleet Esq, Lord of the Manor of Tewin (who was son and heir of Sir John Fleet, Lord Mayor of London in 1692-3), but he died in 1733. His childless widow erected a memorial in Tewin church. Next she married a neighbour, Colonel Sabine, of Queen Hoo Hall. His elder brother General Sabine, Governor of Gibraltar, owned the estate adjoining hers of Tewinbury. Poor Mrs Sabine was soon widowed again, but in 1739 she made a still more advantageous match with the Rt Hon. Charles, 8th Baron Cathcart (c.1686-1740), himself a widower. A Scottish aristocrat, he had been appointed equerry to King George I in 1730 and succeeded to the peerage two years later.[2] Subsequently he was made governor of Londonderry and commander-in-chief of the British forces in America and the West Indies, alongside Admiral Vernon, dying of endemic fever at Dominica in 1740.

For love – by her own later account – or perhaps rather from infatuation – but unwisely as it turned out, Elizabeth married five years later Hugh Macguire, a dashing young subaltern from County Fermanagh, who had been in the service of the Empress Maria Theresa of Hungary. She purchased him a colonel's commission in the army. Scarcely was their honeymoon over when this young blood, after obtaining all the money and personal property of hers on which he could lay hands and having with the assistance of a mistress (who had insinuated herself into Lady Cathcart's confidence) got possession of her will, endeavoured, by holding a pistol to her head to obtain her title-deeds and to make her sign a document that he had drawn up conveying to him the reversion of all her estates! Thwarted in this foul attempt, Macguire determined to abduct her to Ireland in order to obtain absolute control over all her property. She however, getting wind of this, plaited under her hair and quilted into her petticoat all her diamonds before she was forcibly removed to Holyhead.

Her friends appealed to the Lord Chief Justice for a Writ of Habeas Corpus and sent it with an attorney to pursue the fugitives, but when he caught up with them Macguire calmly produced his mistress (in place of Lady Cathcart), who told him that she was travelling to Ireland of her own free will. As the attorney was returning to London in dismay, Macguire sent two highwaymen after him, who stole the writ. Thus he carried Elizabeth off to his native County Fermanagh and confined her for twenty years in the ruined Castle Nugent on the shores of Lough Erne in County Meath, eight miles from Tempo, which belonged to his family. His victim, amazingly, succeeded in concealing from him her jewels and the whereabouts of the titledeeds of her estate until, eventually, her evil captor was killed (1766), apparently attempting to get the deeds out of a secret cupboard in Tewin Water. Whereupon Lady Cathcart's bailiff went to Ireland and escorted her safely home. Even then she had to regain her home from a third party to whom Macguire had conveyed it by legal proceedings. Thereafter, one learns, she became extremely charitable and munificent in her old age, selling all her estates (to Lord Cowper), and bequeathing generous legacies to god-children and step-children (for she remained childless), as well as to friends, servants and the poor of Tewin, before passing away on 3 August 1789, at the grand old age of ninety-eight.

Lady Cathcart told Mrs Thrale that her first marriage had been to please her parents, her second for money and her third for rank. Her fourth marriage she admitted was for love and had been the worst of all.

It will be noted that, if this medallion does indeed represent 'Lady Cathcart', she would, at the time it was carved (*ie* before Le Marchand's death in 1726), have been simply 'Miss Elizabeth Malyn', or, 'Mrs. James Fleet', for the date of her (first) marriage is not recorded. Given her date of birth *c.*1691, and her appearance in this portrait as a woman of between twenty and thirty years old, it may have been executed to commemorate their wedding, at some time between, say, 1712 and 1722 (date of Le Marchand's last recorded portrait).[3]

1 I am grateful to my daughter, Victoria, for her research into this 'lead'
2 For his portrait in a mezzotint engraving by John Faber after Allan Ramsay, see R. E. Hutchinson, *The Jacobite Rising of 1715*, exh.cat. National Gallery of Scotland, Edinburgh, 1965, pl. opp. p.25
3 There is a possibility, if the title on the label is correct, but the literary reference erroneous, that the sitter might be instead the *first* Lady Cathcart, née Marion Schaw, who died in 1733, leaving the 8th Baron a widower, free to marry in 1739 Elizabeth Fleet (as she then was), who was widowed in the same year.

73*
Elizabeth Eyre (1659-1705) 1700
Portrait medallion; profile to the left
9.5 × 8.25 ($3\frac{3}{4} \times 3\frac{1}{4}$)
The Fitzwilliam Museum, Cambridge (M.12/1946)
Condition: excellent
Inscr: (on the reverse) DOMINA ELIZABETHA EYRE MDCC/DLM/F

PROV: The Rt Hon. Lord Chesham (his sale, Sotheby's, 10 December 1946, lot 73); Given by The Friends of the Fitzwilliam Museum

LIT: W. Musgrave (ed. G. J. Armytage), *Obituary . . .* II, London, 1900, p.290; Houfe, 1971, p.70, fig.6

Other example: see Cat.73a

Elizabeth Eyre was the daughter of Sir Anthony Chester of Chichely and the wife of Charles Nicholas Eyre (see Cat.74).[1] She is buried in Salisbury Cathedral.[2] Le Marchand carved in the same year a portrait of a little boy, who was probably her son, for he was called Charles Chester Eyre (Cat.75). An anonymous young lady initialled, but not dated, by Le Marchand may be a daughter (Cat.76).

1 In the museum records she is identified as probably Elizabeth, née Rudge, wife of Sir Robert Eyre (1666-1735), Judge of the Queen's Bench, and this is not impossible. However, if she is mother of the boy on the medallion in the Victoria & Albert Museum that is also dated 1700, who is called Charles Chester Eyre (Cat.75), she is not that Elizabeth, for none of Robert Eyre's children bore these christian names (*Landed Gentry*, under 'Eyre Matcham of Newhouse')
2 Le Neve, *Monumenta Anglicana, III, 1700-1715*, London, 1717, p.100: the inscription was recorded by Francis Bird, so it may have been his work, but the sculpture no longer exists. My thanks to Mr John Lord of Lincoln for this information and for other insights into the Eyre family and their relationships with other patrons of Le Marchand

73a*
Elizabeth Eyre (1659-1705) *c.*1770
Wax portrait medallion; profile to the left
9.5 × 8.25 ($3\frac{3}{4} \times 3\frac{1}{4}$)
Wedgwood Museum, Barlaston (No.2421)
Inscr: (on the reverse) DOMINA ELIZABETHA EYRE MDCC/DLM/F.

PROV: Old factory site

Other example: see Cat.73

74*
After Le Marchand
Charles Nicholas Eyre (d.1713) (?) *c.*1770
Wax portrait medallion; profile to the right
7.5 × 6.5 ($3 \times 2\frac{1}{8}$); when complete, identical to Cat.73
Wedgwood Museum, Barlaston (No.2443)
Condition: fragmentary

PROV: Old factory site

72

73

73a

This wax medallion is too damaged to measure meaningfully, but it has the same incised border moulding and curvature in the preserved segment of the rim at right as on the Wedgwood wax cast of Elizabeth Eyre (Cat.73a).

The basis for the hypothetical identification of the author and subject of the wax at Wedgwood is its similarity to the cast of Elizabeth, and the fact that their size, style, border, and depth of carving are so close.

The putative subject was a Gentleman of the Privy Chamber and Cup-bearer to Queen Anne.

75*
Charles Chester Eyre (d.1713) (?) 1700
Portrait medallion; profile to the right
9.3 × 7.9 ($3\frac{5}{8}$ × $3\frac{1}{8}$)
The Victoria & Albert Museum, London, A.19-1974
Condition: good
Inscr: (on the reverse, with (?) the outline of a coffin) CAROLUS CHESTER / EYRE ARM. / 1700 / D.L.M.

PROV: Mrs M. H. B. Macnab; Sotheby's, 1 July 1974, lot 130; R. G. Coats, London, 1974; Museum purchase (Hildburgh Bequest)

EXH: Victoria & Albert Museum, London, *Objects: The V&A Collects. 1974-1978*

LIT: Reilly and Savage, 1973, p.349

Other example: see Cat.75a

The elegantly attired seven-year-old boy, who may have died young (if the design on the reverse represents a coffin), was almost certainly a son of Elizabeth Eyre, whose portrait was dated in the same year, 1700 (see Cat.73), and her husband, Charles Nicholas Eyre (Cat.74). Elizabeth's maiden name was Chester, for her father was Sir Anthony Chester, and this explains the boy's middle name. He is believed to have waited upon Queen Anne. The presence of a mould at Wedgwood's, where there are

also moulds of Elizabeth Eyre (Cat.73a) and, possibly, of her husband (Cat.74) strengthens the likelihood of a filial relationship between the boy and Mrs Eyre.

75a
Charles Chester Eyre (d.1713) (?) *c.*1770
Wax portrait medallion; profile to the right
9.3 × 7.9 ($3\frac{5}{8}$ × $3\frac{1}{8}$)
Wedgwood Museum, Barlaston

PROV: Old factory site

LIT: Reilly and Savage, 1973, p.349

Other example: see Cat.75

76*
Anonymous Lady (possibly of the Eyre family) *c.*1700 (?)
Portrait medallion; profile to the right
10.3 × 8.25 ($4\frac{1}{16}$ × $3\frac{1}{4}$)
Herr Reiner Winkler, Wiesbaden (bought London, 1975)
Condition: repaired crack in ground, otherwise good
Inscr: (on the ground below the truncation) D.L.M.F.

PROV: R. G. Coats, London

EXH: Deutsches Elfenbeinmuseum, *Aus der Elfenbeinkunst der Welt*, exh.cat. Erbach i. O., 1976, no.273

LIT: Theuerkauff, 1984, pp.89-90, no.46

This is a charming and characteristic portrait of a young lady of perhaps twenty-five years old, *en déshabillé*. For a full discussion of her stylistic affinities with other portraits of ladies by Le Marchand, see Theuerkauff, 1984.

There seems to be in the profile of her face a family likeness to the portrait of Charles Chester Eyre (Cat.75), and this may provide a clue as

74

75

76

to her identity. Perhaps she was an elder sister. Her face is also consistent with Le Marchand's medallion of Elizabeth Eyre (Cat.73), who may be their mother. If that is the case, the present medallion may date from around 1700, when both the others were dated.

77*
Anne Nelthorpe, née Hobson (Life dates not known) 1701
Bust
14 (5½)
Private Collection
Condition: slight cracking
Inscr: (on reverse) LE/MARCHAND/FE. / 1701

PROV: By family descent

EXH: Museum of London 1985, no.306, p.210

This lady is presumed to be a member of the Nelthorpe family, who still own it,[1] and as Tessa Murdoch writes in the catalogue of 1985 (cited above): 'who although they were based in Lincolnshire had strong London connections in this period. Richard Nelthorpe (1667-1731) worked as a goldsmith in Lombard Street, London and John Nelthorpe (b.1663) was an Aleppo merchant. The most likely sitter would be Anne, only daughter and heir of Sir Nathaniel Hobson of Siceston (alias Siston or Syston) in Lincolnshire, (married 1695; re-married 1703). Henry (b.1661 and a strong Whig) died in 1698, and the next year his widow re-married, to Paris Slaughter (d.1703). Although there were no children by this second marriage, Anne had two sons by Henry Nelthorpe. Thus, although the bust was probably commissioned by Paris Slaughter, it subsequently passed to the Nelthorpes.'

It is interesting to note that a signatory to their marriage settlement in 1695 was John Stukeley, father of the Revd Dr William, another of Le Marchand's sitters much later on (1722: Cat.54). Furthermore, the Nelthorpes were intimately connected at the time with the family of Sir Robert Sutton (d.1746) and he was married to Judith, Countess of Sunderland, thus making a connection with other patrons of the carver, the Churchills and their daughter Anne, who married Charles, Earl of Sunderland (Cats 21-6). On the other hand, this bust may represent the wife of the goldsmith, Richard Nelthorpe, but her identity has not yet been revealed.

The Nelthorpes were also distantly connected with the Eyres (see Cats 73-4), who were sympathetic to the Huguenots, having dealt in wool with their weavers as early as the end of the sixteenth century, and – more recently – members of their extended family circle patronised a Huguenot painter and a silversmith.

A business connection between the Eyres and the Nelthorpes and another of Le Marchand's (putative) patrons, Sir Humphry Morice (Cat.71), is attested by a letter written in 1720 to the latter from Sir Robert Walpole, now in the Bank of England Archive.[2]

1 I am grateful to Mr John Lord of Lincoln for drawing this bust to my attention and continuing to ponder the identity of the sitter, as well as explaining to me some of the ramifications of the family and its links with others who patronised Le Marchand
2 Bank of England Archive; COU. No. B.151/3: typescript, *Transcript of Letters 1701-31 addressed to Humphry Morice* ed. W. Marston Acres FRHS, p.564, Letter no. CCCLXXXII:

> Houghton, June 17th, 1720
>
> Dear Sir,
> Since I saw you I have been desired by two gentlemen to recommend them to you to be admitted into your undertaking for carrying on the African Trade for two thousand pounds each. They are *James Nelthorpe & Kingsmill Eyre*, Esq.† If you will be pleased to subscribe for them, I will upon my return pay you the porportion of their subscription that is now to be paid, & thank you for your civility.
> I am, Dear Humphry, Your most affect. & faithfull Servant, R. WALPOLE

† Secretary of Chelsea Hospital, see *London Gazette*, 19 December 1727

78*
Anonymous Gentleman 1704
Bust
23.5 × 18 × 11 (9¼ × 7 × 4¼)
Private Collection
Condition: cracked and chipped in several places
Inscr: (on pillar at back) DA-D. LE MARCHAND/FET. /1704

77

78

PROV: (?) By family descent

It was traditionally supposed within the family that this very imposing bust might have shown Lord Somers (1651-1716), but such an identification is out of the question, as is proven by comparison with the other bust of that sitter, carved two years later, which is now in Wimpole Hall, Cambridgeshire (Cat.37).

It has been observed that the subject suffered from Bell's palsy on the left side of his face. His identity is at present a mystery, and as he does not resemble Somers, the assumed provenance is not necessarily the right one. Indeed he may not be one of the Somersets at all. There is some likeness to Sir James Thornhill, 'our English History painter of greatest Fame' (G. Vertue), as depicted by Highmore (see J. Harris, 'Harley, the Patriot Collector', in *Apollo*, September, 1985, p.201, fig.5), though it is not compelling. Nonetheless, as Highmore also painted Le Marchand and the Rapers as well, there may be a connection.

Another potential candidate is Sidney, 1st Earl of Godolphin, Lord High Treasurer of England, as painted by Kneller, with whom Le Marchand also worked. (D. Green, *Queen Anne*, London, 1970, pls between pp.40-1).

79
Anonymous Man 1700-20
Bust
23.5×16.25 ($10 \times 6\frac{1}{2}$)
Costantino Collection
Condition: cracks, notably on face

PROV: Mrs Arturo Costantino, The Connoisseur Inc, New York (purchased London before 1976 as part of her private collection); By family descent

The bust has traditionally been regarded as a portrait of Joseph Addison, and it does correspond broadly with Kneller's painting as engraved in 1748 by Houbraken (Victoria & Albert Museum Print Room, E.1703-1960). However, it also resembles Sir John Vanbrugh (1664-1726; National Portrait Gallery, no.3231), though the likeness in neither case is at all compelling.

Though neither signed nor dated, the deeply indented modelling of the folds of the cloak and treatment of the long wig are distinctive for Le Marchand's authorship. The handling of the facial features, with rather a flattened plane to the forehead, cheeks and chin and with the nose projecting strongly from it, recalls that of the Anonymous Nobleman which is signed and dated 1700 (Cat.29). This may therefore be among the carver's earlier busts, and the absence of signature may result from its having been paired with another bust that would have faced towards the strongly turned head, perhaps representing his wife and posed rather like that supposedly showing Anne Nelthorpe, which is signed and dated 1701 (Cat.77).

80*
Anonymous Man 1700-20
Portrait medallion; profile to the right
13 ($5\frac{1}{8}$)
The British Museum, London, No.459
Condition: good
Inscr: (on the ground below the truncation) D.L.M.F.

PROV: Gibson Craig sale, Christie's, April 1887; Given by A.W. Franks Esq, 1887

LIT: Maskell, 1905, pl.LXVI; Dalton, 1909, no.459, pl.CI

79

80

81

81*
Anonymous Man 1700-20
Portrait medallion; profile to the right
7 ($2\frac{3}{4}$)
The British Museum, London, No.461
Condition: some damage to the ground, although the image of the sitter is intact
Inscr: (on the ground below the truncation) D.L.M.F.

PROV: Given by A.W. Franks Esq, in 1879

LIT: Dalton, 1909, no.461, p.152, pl.CIII

82*
Anonymous Lady 1700-20
Portrait medallion; full-frontal
18.1 × 15 ($7\frac{1}{8} \times 5\frac{7}{8}$)
The Fitzwilliam Museum, Cambridge (M.6.1945)
Condition: minor cracks in ground.
Inscr: (on the ground below the truncation) D.L.M.

PROV: Bought in Dublin (see red label on the reverse); Given by Mrs W. D. Dickson

LIT: Houfe, 1971, p.70, no.13

The medallion is a near-pair to, and has always been with, Cat.683, so that a family relationship may be inferred, perhaps that of mother and son.

They share the large size of medallion, the considerable depth and height of the image, as well as turning their heads slightly towards one another and having the opposite hand fingering their drapery. It is not known whether their provenance from Dublin indicates that the sitters are Irish or Anglo-Irish, but at least one other of Le Marchand's sitters was Irish, John Vesey Archbishop of Tuam and his bust used to be in Ireland (Cat.38).

83*
Anonymous Young Man 1700-20
Portrait medallion; nearly frontal
21.7 × 16 ($8\frac{1}{2} \times 6\frac{1}{4}$)
The Fitzwilliam Museum, Cambridge (M.5.1945)
Condition: excellent
Inscr: (on the ground below the truncation) D.L.M.F.

PROV: Bought Dublin (red label on the back); Given by Mrs W. D. Dickson to the Fitzwilliam Museum (in 1945?)

LIT: Houfe, 1971, p.70, no.13

The medallion is a near pair to, and has always been with, Cat.82, so that a family relationship may be inferred, perhaps that of son and mother.

The half-length bust is an unusual format for Le Marchand, with the left hand of the sitter partly lost in the opening of his robe. The gesture is not unlike that in his cut-out relief that possibly represents Sir Humphry Morice (Cat.71).

84*
Anonymous Young Lady *c*.1720
Portrait medallion; profile to the left
7.8 ($3\frac{1}{16}$)
Edric Van Vredenburgh Collection
Condition: good

PROV: Christie's, 20 April 1988, lot 76

This unpublished ivory medallion – though unsigned – is positively attributable to Le Marchand owing to its type and style. It fits well in the series of female portraits by the carver, though it is unique among the ladies in its severe truncation and absence of drapery. However, this deliberately classical arrangement may be paralleled in Le Marchand's

82

83

84

medallion of 1722 showing the Reverend William Stukeley (Cat.54). The placing of the head on the circular ground and the clarity of its medallic profile are masterly, suggesting that this may be a late work too. Perhaps the subject was a lady of classical learning, an early 'blue stocking'?

It is most similar to an almost circular medallion of Lady Elizabeth Eyre (1700) in the Fitzwilliam Museum, Cambridge (Cat.73): the treatment of the eye and drilling of the pupil, together with the mouth and chin, are remarkably alike. An oval portrait of a young lady *en déshabillé* in the Winkler Collection also exhibits a similar treatment of the facial features (Cat.76; Theuerkauff, 1984, pp.89-90, no.46); as does the plaque of Anne Dacier in the British Museum (Cat.55).

85*
Anonymous Nobleman 1700-20
Portrait medallion; profile to the right
12.75 (5)
R. T. Gwynn Collection
Condition: slightly discoloured and cracks at the base
Inscr: (on the ground below the truncation) D.M.; (in ink, scarcely legible, on the verso) 'Duke . . .'.

PROV: E. L. Paget Collection (sold Sotheby's, 11 October 1949, lot 83, pl.XII); Bought by W. L. Hildburgh, for presentation to the Victoria & Albert Museum, but instead exchanged against the following lot, no.84, depicting the Duke of Marlborough (Cat.21), with the dealer Alfred Spero, who had purchased it at the sale; Purchased from Spero by the present owner

The fact that this medallion was in the Paget Collection together with the one showing the Duke of Marlborough is hard to interpret. They could have been purchased by Paget quite separately, and were then simply placed by Sotheby's in successive lots, owing to their similarity of material and authorship.

On the other hand, both are of similar size and so might be part of a

series (though this is about the standard size for plaques from the carver's maturity). The present sitter looks younger and fatter than John Churchill. If there is a familial connection between the subjects of the two plaques, and if the title noted on the verso of the present one is *in*accurately recorded, the subject could perhaps be Charles 3rd Earl of Sunderland, Marlborough's son-in-law from 1699.

Failing this, the slightly aquiline and sharply pointed nose, well-formed lips, small, projecting lower jaw-bone and double-chin are not unlike those of the celebrated collector, Edward Harley, 2nd Earl of Oxford (1689-1741) in portraits by Kneller and Richardson (National Portrait Gallery, London, no.1808; for the latter see J. Harris, 'Harley, the Patriot Collector', in *Apollo*, September, 1985, p.198, fig.1). The Earl was certainly aware of Le Marchand, for in 1739 he bought at Lord Halifax's sale the ivory bust of Lord Somers (Cat.37). In view of the present sitter's age, if it depicts Harley, it could not have been carved before *c.*1710.

86
Anonymous Man 1700-20
Portrait medallion; profile to the right
12 (4¾)
David T. Owsley Collection, New York
Condition: slight cracking
Inscr: (on the ground below the truncation) D.L.M.

PROV: David Peel, exh.cat., 1967, no.2 repr.; Private Collection; (Sotheby's, New York, 21 May 1982, lot 148; unsold)

87*
After Le Marchand
Anonymous Man *c.*1770
Wax portrait medallion; profile to the left
12.7 × 10.2 × 2.5 (5 × 4 × 1)
Wedgwood Museum, Barlaston (No.2505)
Condition: loss to upper right segment of ground

85

86

There is no trace of a signature on the obverse. The original ivory, from which this was cast, was deeply carved. The flatness under the curve of the truncation may not reflect the original, but would have been filled in before casting, in order to avoid an undercut, which would have prevented the casts coming cleanly out of the plaster mould.

88*
Anonymous Man *c.*1770
Wax portrait medallion; profile to the right
8.5×7 ($3\frac{3}{8} \times 2\frac{3}{4}$)
Wedgwood Museum, Barlaston (No.2410)
INSCR: (on the reverse) Le Marchand

Other example: there is another cast, inferior in definition, at Barlaston (No.2409)

89*
Anonymous Man *c.*1770
Wax portrait medallion; profile to the left
$10.8 \times 8.5 \times 2$ ($4\frac{1}{4} \times 3\frac{3}{8} \times \frac{3}{4}$)
Wedgwood Museum, Barlaston (No.2470)

The drapery is modelled in folds under the truncation, and as a whole the medallion is deeply carved. This portrait is one of only three where the profile faces left, the others being Cats 14, 61. It is close in size to the wax cast medallion of a lady (Cat.22), also in the Wedgwood Museum, that has been identified here tentatively as Sarah, Duchess of Marlborough, but the subject is not the Duke, while he faces the same way as she does. He might therefore be a relative of the Churchills, or a

member of the Raper family, who consititute the subjects of the majority of the plaster moulds at Barlaston.

90*
Anonymous Man *c.*1770
Wax portrait medallion; profile to the right
$11 \times 9.5 \times 2$ ($4\frac{3}{8} \times 3\frac{3}{4} \times \frac{3}{4}$)
Wedgwood Museum, Barlaston (No.2384)
Condition: loss to far right segment of ground

There is no trace of a signature on the obverse. The folds of the drapery are modelled under the truncation.

91*
After a model attributed to David Le Marchand
Anonymous Knight of the Order of the Garter, perhaps Robert Walpole, 1st Earl of Orford, Prime Minister (1676-1745) *c.*1770
Wax portrait medallion; profile three-quarters to the left
10.1×8.8 ($4 \times 3\frac{1}{2}$)
Wedgwood Museum, Barlaston (No.2418)

The sitter is depicted in a lace jabot, ermine cape and the chain of the Order. The square-set features, jowls and double chin relate well to Kneller's portrait of Walpole in the 1720s. A possible documentary link between this eminent subject and others of Le Marchand's patrons is in a letter of 1720 (see Cat.77, note 2).

However, in the absence of David's usual sinuous and idiosyncratically carved drapery, an attribution to him is less secure, and in view of the length of time Walpole survived him, other candidates for its authorship, such as Isaac Gosset, should be borne in mind.

91

88 and 89

Figure Sculpture and Narrative Reliefs

Sculpture in the round and narrative reliefs signed by Le Marchand are rarer than those by most continental ivory carvers. Of his religious subjects, the *Crucified Christ* from the Victoria & Albert Museum is the most beautiful, and of the classical, mythological ones, the figurine of *Apollo* from Alnwick Castle is very delicate, though the *Venus and Cupid* is more substantial and traditional in appearance. A relief of *Apollo and the Muses on Mount Parnassus*, though unsigned, conforms well in style with the figurine of *Apollo* (and with another similar one in Darmstadt), as well as with David's relief of *The Miracle of Christ healing the Man with the Withered Hand* from Cardiff (see Cat.66).

92
The Virgin and Child Date unknown
Ivory statuette
17.5 (6⅞)
The Museum of Art and Archaeology, University of Missouri, Columbia, Mo. (Acc.No.69.1023)
Condition: severely cracked along the grain of the tusk and darkened: right forearm and right foot of the child are missing. Two holes are drilled through the flange of the base for affixing
Inscr: (on the reverse at the base in 'manuscript') Da-d Le Marchand

PROV: Gift of Miss Sarah Catherine France in honor of her brother Charles B. France

LIT: Foah, 1974, pp.38-43; Avery, 1984, p.116, pl.xix b

The *Virgin and Child* had been one of the most universally popular subjects to be carved in ivory since the Middle Ages, and the generally tapering form of a heavily draped standing woman was very appropriate for carving out of the solid tip of a tusk. Indeed, the distinct curve of the elephant's tusk may have been the origin of the swaying pose so typical of Gothic carvings of this theme. It remained a staple product of the Dieppe ivory carvers until after Le Marchand's day, for example in the *oeuvre* of the Belleteste dynasty of the later eighteenth century.

It is not certain at what date David might have carved this image, though there is a presumption that it might have been before he left his native France, if that was not in 1685, but slightly later, for example after he carved the image of Vauban in 1689, but before appearing in Edinburgh in 1696. Le Marchand introduces a novel idea, inasmuch as the Virgin appears to be offering the Child to the beholder, as distinct from merely holding him to her side, as was traditional. The imagery would not have found great favour with British Protestants at the period, though of course it may have been carved covertly for a recusant family, or a Jacobite patron.

Le Marchand's representation has the heavier swathes of drapery characteristic of Baroque renderings in France and one might compare the more heavily-built group in terracotta of 1710 by his near-

contemporary, P.-J. Hardy (1653-1737).[1] The restrictions imposed by the shape of the tusk – a slightly tapering and bending cylinder – may be remarked, though the carver managed to minimise their aesthetic effect. Similar problems had been encountered when carving two larger figures of the *Mourning Virgin* and *St John the Evangelist* by his predecessor, Pierre-Simon Jaillot (*c*.1631-81): these were to flank a *Crucifix*, his *morceau de réception* for the Académie royale in Paris (1664).[2] Here, the Virgin, not encumbered by the Child by virtue of the different subject, is – generally speaking – similar in handling and appearance to Le Marchand's group, and it may be assumed that he was familiar with such pieces from his childhood in France.

1 C. Avery and A. Laing, *Fingerprints of the Artist: European Terra-Cotta Sculpture from the Arthur M. Sackler Collections*, Cambridge, Mass., 1980, pp.162-3; F. Souchal, *French Sculptors of the 17th and 18th centuries: The reign of Louis XIV*, 1, Oxford, 1977, pp.118-19, no.63
2 Formerly Lord Astor, Hever Castle collection, sold Sotheby's 6 May 1983, lot 332, and purchased by the Victoria & Albert Museum (M. Baker, 'Baroque Ivory Carving in France and England', in *National Art-Collecitons Fund Review*, 1984, pp.106-7)

93* (Plate 6)
Crucified Christ Date unknown, probably after 1700
Ivory statue
39.5 × 27 (15½ × 10⅝)
The Victoria & Albert Museum, London, A.42-1983 (acquired with the assistance of the National Art-Collections Fund)
Condition: minor cracks; otherwise excellent
Inscr: (on the reverse, at the bottom of the loin-cloth) D.L.M.F.

PROV: Sale at Tyttenhanger House, Hertfordshire, former home of the Earl of Caledon; Purchased by Mr Lindley; Sold by private treaty through Christie's to the Victoria & Albert Museum, 1983 (£32,760)

LIT: Foah, 1974, pp.38-43; *Christie's Review of the Year*, 1983, pp.14, 16; Avery, 1984, pp.116-17, pl.xx (b); Baker, 1984, pp.106-7

This superb and movingly portrayed Crucifix figure is the most impressive of David's three surviving religious works (see Cats 66, 92). It is interesting to note that as a Huguenot he felt free to carve this highly emotive subject, and apparently in the fraught circumstances in which he lived in this country, for it might have seemed a rather 'Popish image' to the prejudiced Protestant of those days. Possibly it was carved covertly for a Catholic recusant and/or a Jacobite.

Le Marchand dwells on the anatomy of the ideal male torso, but does not omit to endow the features of Christ with an expression of profound pathos. He exploited the tricky details of the crown of thorns to demonstrate his technical virtuosity by intricate undercutting, while the mouth too is deeply excavated with the drill. As Malcolm Baker has written, 'The subtly modelled musculature of the torso and the heavily bunched draperies of the loin cloth give the figure a monumentality unusual for its size'.

Here too, as in the case of the *Virgin and Child*, a valid comparison may be made with a work of an immediate predecessor, Pierre-Simon Jaillot (*c*.1631-81), whose magnificent ivory Crucifix dated 1664 was his *morceau de réception* for the Académie royale.[1] That image of the Corpus Christi is in the Jansenist position, with arms raised more vertically and feet nailed separately, side by side, rather than as here overlapped and held by a single nail.

1 See Baker, 1984

94
Attributed to Le Marchand
Charity Date unknown
Rectangular ivory plaque
13.5×8.2 $\left(5\frac{5}{16} \times 3\frac{1}{4}\right)$
The Kestner-Museum, Hannover (Inv.No.446)
Condition: cracked

PROV: Friedrich Culemann (1811-1886), Hannover – school governor and proprietor of a book-printing works; Purchased for the Kestner-Museum, 1887[1]

LIT: Theuerkauff, 1984, p.92, n.10

While the subject – in view of the composition – might be mistaken for the *Virgin and Child with the Infant St John*, the inclusion of a third child, without the wings of a cherub, and the absence of the standard attributes of a lamb and reed cross to identify St John makes it more likely to be a representation of Charity. That principal Christian Virtue is usually

93

92

92

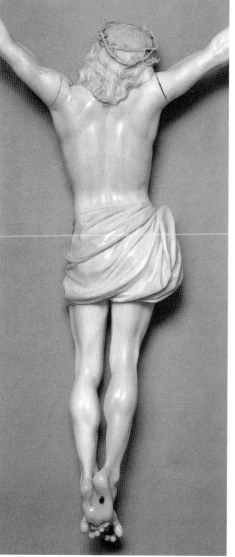

93

shown standing, but can be seated, with three infants, and is depicted frequently as suckling one, while the others reach up for her attention.

A connection with Le Marchand was suggested in 1984 by Dr Christian Theuerkauff of the Staatliche Museen, Berlin, when first he drew the panel to the author's attention, and in one's present state of knowledge about the carver's figurative work, this seems an acceptable attribution. The drapery style and facial types are consistent with Le Marchand's signed group of the *Virgin and Child* (Cat.92), as is the flattened rendering of perspective, with steeply sloping, indeed almost vertical, floor, and a minimum of stage properties – here just a simple bench and a stylised curtain.

The artist has cleverly managed to arrange the three small and one large figure all within a containing oval, whose long axis corresponds with one of the diagonals of the whole surface area. Its lower edge is established by the almost continuous curve formed by the contour of the Virgin's left shoulder and arm and then running on down through the hem of her robe; while the notional upper curve of the oval is punctuated dramatically by the three heads, which are interconnected visually and psychologically by significant glances.

1 The author is grateful to colleagues at the Kestner-Museum, originally Dr U. Gehrig, Director, and recently Dr Helga Hilschenz-Mlynek, Senior Curator, for this information, the photograph and their kind permission to reproduce it here

95* (Plate 7)
Venus and Cupid 1710-20
Ivory statuette
33.5 (13)
The Victoria & Albert Museum, London, A.69-1926
Condition: cracked
Inscr: (on the reverse of the base) D. Le Marchand, Scul.

94

PROV: E. Good, 1 New Oxford Street, London W1 (£37 10s)

LIT: Victoria & Albert Museum, *Review*, 1926, p.5, pl.4; *Burlington Magazine*, LIII, 1928, p.249, pl.1, C.D.; Maclagan and Longhurst, 1929, II, p.84

The subject of *Venus and Cupid* was beloved of wood and ivory carvers from the Renaissance onwards for the opportunity of rendering sensuous nudity and demonstrating one's knowledge of antiquity. It also permitted the smaller figure of the boy to be used as a support for the adult, whose ankles alone would otherwise be rather weak to support the body. The warm sheen that ivory can be given, together with its creamy colour, lend themselves particularly well to carving such an image of idealised human nudity. There are therefore many examples by Le Marchand's predecessors, notably from the Flemish school of carvers in the wake of Rubens and Van Dyck.

There may be a connection with one in particular, the group by the German carver, Georg Petel (1601/2 to 1634), that possibly belonged to Rubens himself, and (from 1626) to the Duke of Buckingham.[1] Le Marchand's humanist patron the Reverend William Stukeley (Cat.54) apparently owned a similar group in bronze with eyes inlaid in silver that is now in the Victoria & Albert Museum (A.27-1956). He made a drawing of it in 1724, presuming it to be an antiquity, among some of the actual ancient sculptures belonging to Lord Pembroke at Wilton House. The bronze is slightly smaller than the ivory, and this suggests that it was cast from it, possibly in England. In any case, it is not improbable that Stukeley encouraged Le Marchand to emulate his worthy predecessor's masterpiece in ivory. If this hypothesis is valid, it would suggest a date after 1718, when Stukeley first came to the capital.

However, the connection is by no means secure, and the group may have been carved earlier and for another patron.

1 N. Penny, *Catalogue of European Sculpture in the Ashmolean Museum, 1540 to the Present Day, II, French and Other European Sculpture*, Oxford, 1992, no.361, pp.145-6

96*
Apollo with his lyre, a bow and quiver of arrows 1700-20
Ivory statuette[1]
13 (5⅛)
His Grace The Duke of Northumberland, Alnwick Castle
Condition: the base cracked radially, otherwise reasonably good
Inscr: (on surface of the base) D.L.M.

PROV: By family descent

One of two similar compositions showing the standing god Apollo, signed by Le Marchand (the other being in Darmstadt, Cat.97), this is a rare example of his accomplishment in carving the classical, free-standing figure. David's virtuosity is demonstrated by the undercutting and piercing of the ivory to relieve the limbs and attributes. This must have been done with the help of a drill, so delicate is the work.

The carver here achieves a fine rendering of classical *contrapposto* and shows a great sensitivity to the dynamism of the very refined silhouette when seen from different angles.

1 This ivory was kindly brought to the author's attention by Malcolm Baker, Deputy Head of Research at the Victoria & Albert Museum

97
Apollo 1700-20
Ivory statuette
17.9 (7) without base; 19.5 (8⅝) with base
Hessisches Landesmuseum, Darmstadt (Inv.No.Pl.36:58)
Condition: cracked, particularly in the upper torso; rear volute of lyre missing
Inscr: Scul LE MARCHA.

PROV: From the old noble collection

LIT: Tardy, *Les Ivoires*, Paris, 1966, p.185 repr.; Theuerkauff, 1984, p.92; F. Fischer, *Bildwerke des 17. und 19. Jahrhunderts (Kataloge des Hessischen Landesmuseums*, no.17), Darmstadt, 1991, p.74, no.31, col.pl.IV

Fischer points to several possible prototypes among monumental marble sculptures of the same subject from the Versailles school of sculpture under Louis XIV, and adds that, in view of the distinct turn of the god's head, this statuette may have had a pendant figure of Daphne. He contends that when seen from in front, the figure is composed with

great refinement, even though it expresses an extreme but original stylistic taste.

98*
Attributed to Le Marchand
Apollo and the Muses on Mount Parnassus 1710-20
Rectangular relief
20.2 × 17 × 2.6 (8 × 6¾ × 1)
Herr Reiner Winkler, Wiesbaden
Condition: vertical cracks along the grain to left and right below; there is a grey area and loss parallel with the projecting leg of Apollo

PROV: With Cyril Humphris, London (bought by Herr Winkler on 24 April 1971)

LIT: Theuerkauff, 1984, pp.91-2, no.47

This spectacular plaque has been convincingly attributed to Le Marchand by Dr Christian Theuerkauff of the Staatliche Museen, Berlin, on the grounds of the similarity in style of its many classicising figures

95

96

97

to his signed statuette of the protagonist, *Apollo*, in Darmstadt, to which may now be added the similar and also signed statuette recently discovered in Alnwick Castle (Cats 96-7).

Theuerkauff also adduced its analogies with the relief of Mathew Raper III of 1720 (Cat.64) and with the carver's only extant signed relief of a religious subject, *The Miracle of Christ healing the Man with the Withered Hand* (Cat.66). The comparison with the portrait plaque suggests a latish date in Le Marchand's *oeuvre*,[1] possibly when he was coming under the influence of the classically oriented Dr William Stukeley and other antiquarians of the day.

Theuerkauff enumerates the figures in the scene as follows: Apollo, sits at the apex of the composition, his right hand supporting his lyre on a rock, while he points downwards with his left. He is draped in a fluttering cloak. To the right sits Urania, Muse of Astrology, looking heavenwards and holding a celestial globe in contemporary mounting. The bookish seated female figures to left and right in the foreground are probably Calliope and Melpomene, the Muses of Epic Poetry and of Tragedy. The one seated in the same row playing the lute and singing is perhaps Terpsichore, Muse of Dance, and the one standing at the left with outstretched arms may be Thalia, Muse of Comedy. The two

98

99

100

females seated to the left in the middle ground, one with a pair of wind-instruments in her left hand, and looking at one another are probably Euterpe, Muse of Music, with Clio the one of History. The remaining figures are less easy to distinguish in the absence of typical attributes: one is extinguishing a fire with a jug of water, possibly representing Temperance, while her neighbour holds a rudder, a symbol of Good Government.

1 *Pace* Theuerkauff, who guessed that it might be early: however, the whole question of dating Le Marchand's figurative *oeuvre* is hazardous in the extreme, in the absence of pieces bearing dates

99*

Attributed to Le Marchand
Apollo *c.*1720
Medallion; profile to the right
8×6 ($3\frac{3}{16} \times 2\frac{5}{16}$)
Collection of Michael Hall Esq, London
Condition: cracked and discoloured

LIT: Murdoch, 1984, p.69; Avery, 1985, p.1564

In a posthumous sale of Dr Richard Mead's possessions at Langford's rooms (11 March 1755), lot 32 comprised, 'Heads of *Socrates, Plato, Homer, Cicero* and two of *Medusa,* finely copy'd from the antique, in ivory, by Marchand'. None of these has been identified, but they may prove to be like this classically-inspired medallion, whose technique is related to that of Le Marchand. The wreathed head is distinctly reminiscent of Stukeley's (Cat.54) and both are at present in the same collection, which they may have reached together.

The relative softness of carving around the contour of the face and in the curls of hair, less incisive than is often the case with ivories derived from classical hard-stones or struck medals, is similar to that to be observed in a cast of Scipio Africanus that is in the Wedgwood Museum, in company with some casts after Le Marchand's portraits of contemporaries (see Cat.100). The two attributions are thus independent, and serve to corroborate one another.

100*

After a model attributed to Le Marchand
Scipio Africanus *c.*1770
Wax portrait medallion; profile to the right
10.8×8.6 ($4\frac{1}{4} \times 3\frac{3}{8}$)
Wedgwood Museum, Barlaston (No.2514)

PROV: Old factory site

This cast presumably records an original ivory medallion, like so many in the same holding. The degree of relief and the sinuous flow of the animal-skin headdress are consistent with what one would expect of Le Marchand when asked to carve a subject from antiquity in a classical manner. The delicate carving of the profile and softness in rendering the features, despite the stubble and martial personality, relate this to the actual ivory medallion of *Apollo* (Cat.99), which in turn is to be associated with David's *all'antica* profile of his contemporary patron, the Reverend William Stukeley (Cat.54).

Rejected attribution

101

Double portrait of William and Mary 1689-94, or later
Rectangular portrait plaque; the King facing right, the Queen left, within an irregular, dished background
9.3 ($3\frac{5}{8}$)
Private Collection
Condition: good
Inscr: (lower right corner of surface of the 'frame') D.L.M.

PROV: Sotheby's, 13 December 1979, lot 297

A somewhat similar double portrait appears on a Dutch silver Coronation medal for William and Mary of 1689 by an unidentified artist, the reverse with a scene of Britannia welcoming their arrival and the assistance of Holland (Franks and Gruber, 1885/1904/II pl.LXXII, no.4).

Despite the initials D.L.M. (which are inscribed in italicised capitals that are atypical for Le Marchand), the style of this portrait is far too hard and primitive to be his work, even as a juvenile apprentice – especially now that one knows how good he was by the relevant year, 1689, owing to the emergence of the dated plaque showing possibly Vauban (Cat.1). The dished background would also be unique in his *oeuvre*.

An alternative candidate is his more or less contemporary, though far less able, fellow-countryman, Jean Mancel (*active* pre-1680 to post-1717), who did carve such medallions in a crude approximation of the incisive low-relief work of Jean Cavalier. Indeed, one wonders whether the 'signature' (if not totally false) might not have been cunningly adapted from an honest 'I.M.' for Jean Mancel, to the more prestigious and valuable initials of our carver. Nevertheless, attractive though this hypothesis may be, a medallion in the Winkler Collection that is definitely in Mancel's style and also shows Queen Mary, seems a trifle preferable to the present image of the Queen and her Consort (see Theuerkauff, 1984, pp.88-9, no.45).

101

Bibliography

Avery, C., 'David Le Marchand – Huguenot Ivory Carver (1674-1726)', *Proceedings of the Huguenot Society, London*, XXIV, 2, 1984, pp.113-18, pls XVII-XX.

Avery, C., 'Missing, Presumed Lost: Some Ivory Portraits by David Le Marchand', *Country Life*, 6 June 1985, pp.1562-4.

Baker, M., 'Baroque Ivory Carving in France and England', *National Art-Collections Fund Review*, 1984, pp.106-7.

Burlington Fine Arts Club, *Carvings in Ivory*, London, 1923, exh.cat. (cited as 'BFAC, 1923').

Chennevières-Pointel, C.P. de, *Notes d'un compilateur sur les sculpteurs et les sculptures en ivoire*, Amiens, 1857.

Dalton, O.M., *Catalogue of the Ivory Carvings of the Christian Era in the British Museum*, London, 1909.

Dussieux, L., *Les artistes Français à l'étranger*, 3rd ed., Paris/Lyon, 1876.

Ferment, C., 'Portraits Medallions d'Ivoire', *L'Estampille*, no.157, May 1983, pp.35-47.

Foah, R., 'David Le Marchand's Madonna and Child', in *Muse–Annual of the Museum of Art and Archaeology, University of Missouri – Columbia*, VII, 1974, pp.38-43.

Franks, A.W. and Gruber, H.A., *Medallic Illustrations to British History*, London, 1885, I, p.652, 7; (plates) London, 1904-11, pl.LXIX.

Gjertsen, D., *The Newton Handbook*, London, 1986, p.45.

Hodgkinson, T., 'An Ingenious Man for Carving in Ivory', *Victoria and Albert Museum Bulletin*, I, 2, April 1965, pp.29-32.

Houfe, S., *Sir Albert Richardson, The Professor*, Luton, 1980, pp.151-2, 157.

Houfe, S.R., 'A Whig Artist in Ivory, David Le Marchand (1674-1726)', *The Antique Collector*, April 1971, p.66.

Julius, A., *J. Cavalier och nagra andra Elfenbenssnidare . . .* , Uppsala, 1926, p.88f.

Kerslake, J., 'Sculptor and Patron? Two Portraits by Highmore', *Apollo*, XCV, January 1972, pp.25-9.

Lami, S., *Dictionnaire des sculpteurs de l'école française sous le règne de Louis XIV*, Paris, 1906.

Longhurst, M., *English Ivories*, London, 1926.

Maclagan, E. and Longhurst, M., *Catalogue of Carvings in Ivory*, Victoria & Albert Museum, London, 1929, II, p.84, pls LXXI-II.

Maskell, A., *Ivories*, London, 1905, pp.385-7, pl.LXVI.

Maze-Sencier, A., *Le Livre des Collectionneurs*, Paris, 1885.

Milet, A., 'Ivoires et Ivoiriers de Dieppe', *L'Art*, LXIV, 1905, pp.210-11.

Murdoch, T., *The Quiet Conquest: The Huguenots 1685 to 1985*, exh.cat., Museum of London, 1985, pp.208-12, nos 303-10 (cited as 'Museum of London').

Murdoch, T., 'Some Huguenot Craftsmen from Dieppe in London', in *Seventeenth Century French Studies VI*, 1984, pp.60-74.

Philippovich, E. von, *Elfenbein*, 2nd rev. and enl. ed., Munich, 1982.

Publications of the Huguenot Society ('Quarto Series'), XXVII (1923), p.85; XXVIII (1924), p.22; XXIX (1926), p.90.

Publications of the Huguenot Society ('Quartro Series'), LIII (1977), see 'Le Marchand'.

Reilly, R. and Savage, G., *Wedgwood, the Portrait Medallions*, London, 1973.

Scherer, C., *Elfenbeinplastik seit der Renaissance (Monographien des Kunstgewerbes herausgegeben von Jean Louis Sponsel)*, Leipzig, c.1905, VII, pp.25-6.

Scherer, C., *Die Braunschweiger Elfenbeinsammlung*, Leipzig, 1931.

The Walpole Society, XX, 1933, 'Vertue *Notebooks*', II, pp.47, 69-70; *ibid*, XXII, 1934, 'Vertue *Notebooks*', III, pp.13,17; *ibid*, XXIV, 1936, 'Vertue *Notebooks*', IV, pp.50, 61, 166 (cited as 'Vertue, II, III, IV').

Theuerkauff, C., *Die Bildwerke in Elfenbein des 16.-19. Jahrhunderts*, Berlin, 1986, pp.65, 136, 139, 245, 305, 324.

Theuerkauff, C., *Elfenbein: Sammlung Reiner Winkler*, Munich, 1984, pp.89-92, nos 46-7.

Theuerkauff, C., *Elfenbein: Sammlung Reiner Winkler*, II, Munich, 1994, pp.58-9, no.20, p.160, n.

Thieme, U. and Becker, A., *Lexikon der bildenden Künstler*, Leipzig, XXIII, 1929.

Vertue, see under *The Walpole Society*

Walpole, H. (ed. R.N. Wornum), *Anecdotes of Painting in England*, London, 1849, II, p.625.

Westfall, R.S., *Never at Rest: A Biography of Isaac Newton*, Cambridge, 1980.

Whinney, M.D., *Victoria and Albert Museum; English Sculpture 1720-1830*, London, 1971, nos 1, 2, pp.26-9.

List of Works by Location

All items are in ivory and are portrait medallions, unless otherwise specified. Numbers refer to the Catalogue which also gives the full title of each work

Great Britain

ALNWICK CASTLE
The Duke of Northumberland
96. *Apollo*, statuette

ALTHORP
The Earl Spencer
24. *Anne Sunderland, Countess of Sunderland*, bust

ANGLESEY ABBEY, CAMBRIDGESHIRE
The Fairhaven Collection (The National Trust)
29. *Anonymous Nobleman*, bust

BARLASTON
Wedgwood Museum
22. *Anonymous Lady, possibly Sarah, Duchess of Marlborough* (?), wax
23. *Anonymous Lady*, wax
62b. *Mathew Raper II*, plaster mould
63a. *Mrs Mathew Raper II (née Mary Elizabeth Billers)*, wax
63b. *Mrs Mathew Raper II (née Mary Elizabeth Billers)*, plaster mould
65a. *Moses Raper*, plaster mould
73a. *Elizabeth Eyre*, wax
74. *Charles Nicholas Eyre* (?), wax
87-90. *Anonymous Men*, wax
91. *Anonymous Knight of the Order of the Garter, perhaps Robert Walpole*, wax
100. *Scipio Africanus*, wax

CAMBRIDGE
Fitzwilliam Museum
73. *Elizabeth Eyre*
82. *Anonymous Lady*
83. *Anonymous Young Man*

Greenwich Royal Observatory
52. *John Flamsteed*

CARDIFF
National Museum of Wales
66. *The Miracle of Christ healing the Man with the Withered Hand*, relief

CORSHAM COURT
Trustees of Corsham Estate
45. *Sir Isaac Newton*, wax

DRUMMOND CASTLE
The Grimsthorpe and Drummond Castle Trust
11. *James Drummond, 2nd titular Duke of Perth*
12. *Unidentified Lady of the Drummond family*
13. *The Arms of the Duke of Perth*, circular plaque
14. *King James II of England and VII of Scotland*

EDINBURGH
Royal Museum of Scotland
72. *Lady Cathcart*

LONDON
British Museum
18. *Tenth Earl Marischal* (?)
32. *King George I*
36. *Thomas Brodrick* PC
40. *Samuel Pepys*
53. *Sir Richard Steele*
55. *Anne Dacier*
67. *Sir Christopher Wren*
68. *Sir Isaac Newton*, bust
80. *Anonymous Man*
81. *Anonymous Man*

Christie's (present whereabouts unknown)
J. W. Brett sale, 5 April 1864, lot 2035
46. *Sir Isaac Newton*
sale 1969
61. *David Le Marchand* (?)

Guy's Hospital, The Gordon Museum
43. *Thomas Guy*, wax

Mallett at Bourdon House
33. *King George I*, rectangular plaque

National Portrait Gallery
48. *Sir Christopher Wren*

Lord Thomson of Fleet
71. *Sir Humphry Morice*, bust in deep relief

Mrs M. Wright, 3 Barton Street, London SW1 (last recorded 1936)
69. *John Locke*, bust

Victoria & Albert Museum
3. *Saturn Abducting Cybele*, statuette
4. *Third Earl of Leven*
5. *Countess of Leven*
21. *First Duke of Marlborough*
25. *Anne Churchill, Countess of Sunderland*
31. *King George I*, bust
42. *Thomas Guy*
51. *Charles Marbury*
59. *Gamaliel Voyce*
60. *Mary Voyce*
62a. *Mathew Raper II*, glass paste
64. *Mathew Raper III*

75. *Charles Chester Eyre*
93. *Crucified Christ*, statuette
95. *Venus and Cupid*, statuette

PRIVATE COLLECTIONS, LONDON AND ELSEWHERE
Collection of R.T. Gwynn Esq
85. *Anonymous Nobleman*

Collection of Michael Hall Esq
54. *The Reverend William Stukeley* MD
99. *Apollo*

Collection of Simon Houfe Esq
2. *King Louis XIV*

Lord Thomson of Fleet
71. *Sir Humphry Morice (?)*

Collection of Edric Van Vredenburgh Esq
84. *Anonymous Young Lady*

Anonymous collections
6. *First Earl of Cromartie*
7. *Second Earl of Cromartie*, bust
8. *Sir James Mackenzie of Royston*
9. *Lady Mackenzie of Rosehaugh*
10. *George Mackenzie of Rosehaugh*
28. *Noblewoman sitting with her daughter*, rectangular plaque
38. *Archbishop Vesey*, bust
41. *John Locke*
77. *Anne Nelthorpe*, bust
78. *Anonymous Gentleman*, bust
101. *Double portrait of William and Mary*, rectangular plaque

WIMPOLE HALL
The National Trust
37. *Lord Somers*, bust

WINDSOR CASTLE
The Royal Collection
56. *André Dacier* (?)

Australia

MELBOURNE
The National Gallery of Victoria
47. *Sir Isaac Newton*, bust

Canada

TORONTO
Lord Thomson of Fleet
16. *Anonymous Nobleman*
20. *Queen Anne*
30. *Third Earl of Peterborough*
35. *King George I*
39. *Sir Godfrey Kneller* (?)
44. *Sir Isaac Newton*, rectangular plaque
49. *Christopher Wren Jr Esq* MP
57. *Michael Garnault*
58. *Francis Sambrooke*, bust

69a. *John Locke*, bust 'a'
69c. *John Locke*, bust 'b'
69b. *Sir Isaac Newton*, bust 'a'
69d. *Sir Isaac Newton*, bust 'b'

France

DIEPPE
Château Musée de Dieppe
1. *Maréchal de Vauban* (?)

Germany

BRAUNSCHWEIG
Herzog Anton Ulrich-Museum
34. *King George I*

DARMSTADT
Hessisches Landesmuseum
97. *Apollo*, statuette

HANNOVER
Kestner-Museum
94. *Charity*, rectangular plaque

WIESBADEN-BIEBRICH
Herr Reiner Winkler
50. *Charles Marbury*
76. *Anonymous Lady (possibly of the Eyre family?)*
98. *Apollo and the Muses on Mount Parnassus*, rectangular plaque

Sweden

STOCKHOLM
Nationalmuseum
17. *Anonymous Nobleman*
19. *Man in a Banyan*

Switzerland

ZURICH
Fondation Rau pour le Tiers-Monde
70. *Sir John Houblon (?) formerly called 'Samuel Pepys (?)'*

United States of America

COLUMBIA, MISSOURI
Museum of Art and Archaeology, University of Missouri-Columbia
92. *Virgin and Child*, statuette

NEW YORK
Metropolitan Museum of Art
26. *Anne Churchill, Countess of Sunderland*, bust

Costantino Collection
79. *Anonymous Man (said to be Joseph Addison)*, bust

David Daniels Collection (formerly)
27. *Countess of Berkeley*

David T. Owsley Collection
86. *Anonymous Man*

Bill Gates
Computer Legend

Sara Barton-Wood

Hodder
Wayland

an imprint of Hodder Children's Books

© 2001 White-Thomson Publishing Ltd

Produced by White-Thomson Publishing Ltd
2/3 St Andrew's Place, Lewes, BN7 1UP

Editor: Liz Gogerly
Cover Design: Jan Sterling
Inside Design: Joyce Chester
Picture Research: Shelley Noronha, Glass Onion Pictures
Proofreader: Alison Cooper

Cover: Bill Gates at a Microsoft Press Conference in 1997.

Published in Great Britain in 2001 by Hodder Wayland,
an imprint of Hodder Children's Books
This paperback edition published in 2002

Titles in this series:
Muhammad Ali: The Greatest
Neil Armstrong: The First Man on the Moon
Fidel Castro: Leader of Cuba's Revolution
Diana: The People's Princess
Anne Frank: Voice of Hope
Bill Gates: Computer Legend
Martin Luther King Jr: Civil Rights Hero
Nelson Mandela: Father of Freedom
Mother Teresa: Saint of the Slums
Pope John Paul II: Pope for the People
Queen Elizabeth II: Monarch of Our Times
The Queen Mother: Grandmother of a Nation

British Library Cataloguing in Publication Data
Sara Barton-Wood
  Bill Gates: computer legend. – (Famous lives)
  1. Gates, Bill 2.Businessmen – United States –
  Biography
  3.Computer industry
  I.Title II.Wood, Sara
  338.4'7'005'092

ISBN 0 7502 3883 6

Printed in Hong Kong by Wing King Tong

Hodder Children's Books
An imprint of Hodder Headline Limited
338 Euston Road, London, NW1 3BH

Picture Acknowledgements
The publisher would like to thank the following for giving
permission to use their pictures: Associated Press (title
page), 5, 13, 32, 37, 39 (top), 43, 44; Corbis (cover),
10, 11, 15, 20, 21, 23, 24, 27, 28, 30/ Sygma
© G. Haller, Seattle Post Intelligencer 33/ © Darryl
Heikes 39 (bottom); Robert Harding 14; Lakeside School
8, 9, 12; Microsoft 17, 19, 22, 26, 29; Robert Opie 16
(top and bottom); Photri 7, 25, 31; Pictorial 6;
Popperfoto 4, 34, 35, 36, 38, 40, 41, 42, 45 (top and
bottom); Topham Picturepoint 18.

Contents

Launchpad

It is 24 August 1995. In fifteen marquees on a lawn outside an office in Redmond, Seattle, USA, two and a half thousand guests are drinking champagne. The air is filled with the buzz of excited voices as the guests watch a revolutionary new computer program. This is the launch of Windows 95.

A roar goes up as Bill Gates, President of Microsoft, the company which developed Windows, arrives. He and talk-show host Jay Leno take the stage. They swap jokes about the new technology. Gates claims it will change the way people communicate with each other in the twenty-first century and beyond.

Bill Gates (left) and Jay Leno entertain the world's press at the launch of Windows 95.

A silhouette of Gates on the stage at the Windows' launch.

Gates was right. Sales of the new program soared well over 30 million in its first year. Windows became a household name. The program put 'a computer on every desk and in every home' as Gates had predicted in 1975. That was when he founded his company, at the age of nineteen. This is the story of a computer-mad teenager turned tough businessman who became the world's richest man. And who then gave a great deal of his fortune away to charity.

'People don't want to settle for outdated features or performance. A three-year-old computer is about as popular as a three-year-old newspaper.'
Bill Gates, *The Road Ahead*, 1995.

5

Early Life

Unlike many self-made men, Bill Gates did not have to fight his way up from a poor background. He was born on 28 October 1955 in Seattle, Washington, into a prosperous local business family. His father is a lawyer, his grandfather was a banker. His mother was a teacher before she married and had a family.

Gates was a very strong-willed, active child who liked to rock himself in his cradle and on his toy rocking-horse. Even now, Gates often rocks backwards and forwards, sometimes violently, in his chair. He says it helps him concentrate. Others say it shows that he is slightly autistic.

Star Trek! *This is how people in the 1960s thought the future might look. We are not able to travel in space like the television characters, but computers certainly play a large part in our lives.*

Family life has always been important to him. Gates says that he remembers the atmosphere at home with his parents and two sisters as 'a rich environment in which to learn'. The whole family enjoyed reading, playing board games and cards, especially bridge, and solving puzzles. Winning mattered a great deal! Perhaps this early experience of intense competition prepared him for the cut and thrust of business life later on.

This is the famous Seattle skyline showing the Space Needle (built for the World Fair in 1962), and Mount Rainier in the background.

School

As a schoolboy, Gates was so clever, especially at maths and science, that he did not have to try very hard. The other children teased him because he came top all the time. His easy success and the taunting stopped him making friends. He started making mistakes on purpose to bring his grades down.

His parents realized their son was gifted and decided to move him to a private school in 1967 when he was eleven. Lakeside School had many other outstanding pupils. Gates soon found that he did not come top all the time, even when he was trying.

Lakeside School is like a New England prep school or a British public school with rigid rules and discipline.

Gates in the school's computer room. In the bottom left-hand corner is a teletype machine which connected to a computer via the telephone.

Although Gates was small and shy at this age, he was already extremely competitive. He loved a fast game of tennis, and the thrill of skiing both on water and on snow. He also went on summer camp with friends from Lakeside, where he enjoyed the challenge of outdoor adventures. But what he remembers most vividly from his days at Lakeside was the first time he used a computer. He quickly developed a passion for the machine that was to play such a large part in his life.

Computers before Gates

Small, personal computers with a screen, keyboard and printer, like those in school classrooms today, had not been invented yet. What Gates discovered at Lakeside was a teletype machine. This records information by punching holes on a paper tape. The pattern made by the holes was the earliest form of software. The machine was connected via the telephone to a mainframe computer at a local General Electric office.

Computers were so expensive in the late 1960s that only really big companies could afford them. They were also so big that one computer filled a whole room. So smaller companies, and some schools such as Lakeside, 'bought' time on a computer wherever it was available.

A woman sits at a large computer board at the Gorodok Academy, Centre for Space Studies in the Soviet Union, in 1967.

Nobody at Lakeside, students or teachers, knew how to write the complicated code of holes punched on tape that would tell the computer what to do. But Gates, teaching himself from a handbook, quickly discovered that he could get the computer to solve mathematical puzzles. If he wrote the code correctly, he got a useful answer. If he wrote it wrong, the computer did not understand what was required. It was a challenge he could not resist.

This is how computers looked in the 1950s. Only someone with a real vision of the future, like Gates, could imagine the transformation to today's personal computers .

'The computer I used (at school) was huge and cumbersome and slow and absolutely compelling.'
Bill Gates, from his book *The Road Ahead*, 1995.

The Lakeside Programmers

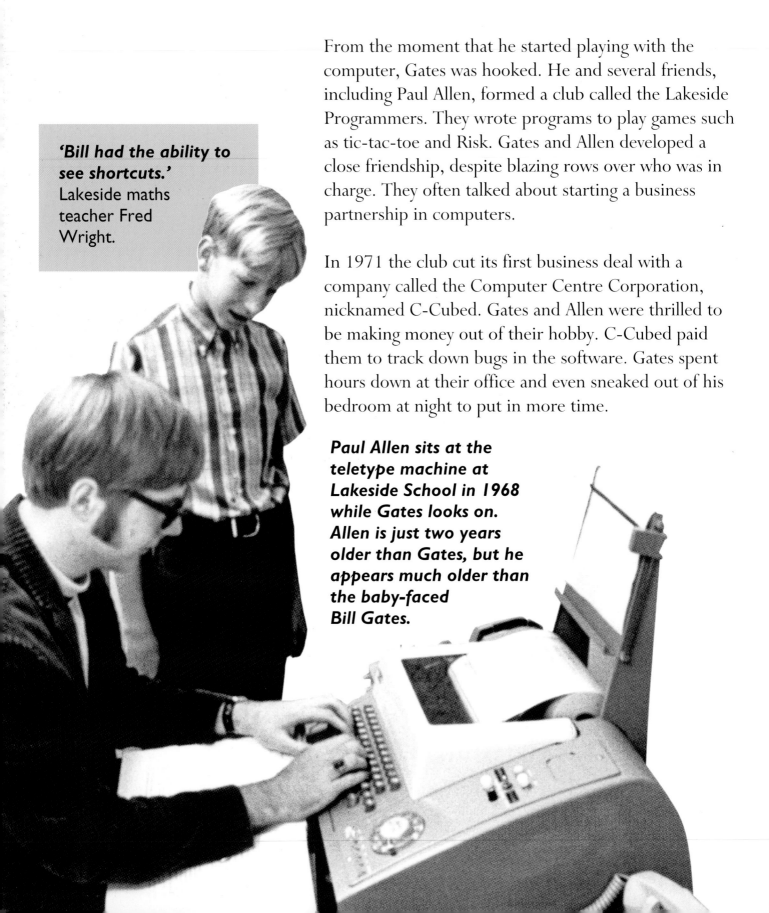

'**Bill had the ability to see shortcuts.**'
Lakeside maths teacher Fred Wright.

From the moment that he started playing with the computer, Gates was hooked. He and several friends, including Paul Allen, formed a club called the Lakeside Programmers. They wrote programs to play games such as tic-tac-toe and Risk. Gates and Allen developed a close friendship, despite blazing rows over who was in charge. They often talked about starting a business partnership in computers.

In 1971 the club cut its first business deal with a company called the Computer Centre Corporation, nicknamed C-Cubed. Gates and Allen were thrilled to be making money out of their hobby. C-Cubed paid them to track down bugs in the software. Gates spent hours down at their office and even sneaked out of his bedroom at night to put in more time.

Paul Allen sits at the teletype machine at Lakeside School in 1968 while Gates looks on. Allen is just two years older than Gates, but he appears much older than the baby-faced Bill Gates.

This is how children at school today learn to use computers. Gates is very keen to give money to schools to buy computers, perhaps because the children will all grow up and buy his products!

Another company paid them $5,000 to write a program to work out weekly pay for their employees. They also wrote programs to analyse information about traffic flow for the police. By now, Gates' school days were coming to an end. With top grades in most subjects, he easily won a place at the top-ranked Harvard University to study maths.

Harvard

The modern science school at Harvard University in Boston, Massachusetts, USA. Gates was outclassed in maths, his chosen subject, so he concentrated on computers instead.

Student life suited Bill Gates, but he lived very irregular hours. Freed from the timetable laid down by home and school, he sometimes went for days without sleep. Living on a diet of pizza and Coke, he often worked for 36 hours without a break. Then he would sleep under the desk.

'I loved my years at college and, in many respects, I regretted leaving. I only did it because I had an idea that couldn't wait.'
Bill Gates, *New York Times*, 8 May 1996.

Gates spent most of his time in the computer centre at Harvard. He worked for weeks on a program for a computer baseball game. This meant using complex mathematical formulae to represent figures hitting, throwing and catching a baseball. Even when he was asleep, he dreamed about computers. A fellow-student remembers hearing him talk in code as he lay on the floor!

He was not at all interested in the social side of university life. Apart from all-night poker sessions or going to a movie, he rarely took time off. Nobody can remember him ever dating a girlfriend at Harvard. But he did make one good friend, Steve Ballmer. Ballmer later joined Microsoft as assistant to the boss.

This is Steve Ballmer speaking at a business conference in 1998. Like Gates, Ballmer can go for days without sleep and is passionate about the computer business.

The Revolution Begins

On a cold winter day in December 1974, in Gates' second year at Harvard, Paul Allen came to visit. As Allen was walking across the university campus, he spotted in a newspaper kiosk the January issue of *Popular Electronics*.
He had read the magazine since he was a schoolboy at Lakeside. On the front cover was a picture of a new computer, the Altair 8800.

Above: ***The first typewriter was made in 1874. It didn't need electricity and it was portable.
In their own way, early typewriters were revolutionary because people could produce print-like documents at work and home.***

Left: ***The electric typewriter was introduced in 1935. It was quicker and more efficient than the earlier typewriters but it was still difficult to correct mistakes.***

ALTAIR 8800 COMPUTER

This is the machine, the Altair 8800, which changed the course of Gates' life and started the computer revolution. In front is a piece of paper tape punched with holes carrying instructions for the machine.

The magazine was advertising the world's first microcomputer. It was a rectangular, metal machine with switches and lights on the front. The magazine's readers could buy the machine in kit form and build their own computer.

> *'We realized that the revolution might happen without us. After we saw that article (in **Popular Electronics**), there was no question of where our life would focus.'*
> Bill Gates quoted in *Bill Gates Speaks* by Janet Lowe, 1998.

Allen's heart pounded with excitement as he bought a copy of the magazine and read the report. He realized at once that this machine marked the start of the computer revolution. It was the moment he and his friend Bill Gates had been waiting for. He rushed off to find Gates, who was playing poker. Allen dragged him away from the game shouting 'Look! Look! It's happening. We've got to do something.'

Blazing a Trail

Albuquerque in New Mexico, USA, is a city in the middle of a desert. After work Gates liked to escape to the sand dunes and drive his car at high speed.

The company making the Altair 8800 was called MITS, based in Albuquerque, New Mexico. MITS needed a computer program to make the machine work. Gates and Allen rang to say they had a program ready. In fact, they did not. But they felt sure they could write one and they were desperate to get in first. They knew lots of other people would be trying to do the same.

'It was a question of whether I could write the program and make it fit into 4K (a very small space in computer sizing) and make it superfast.' [He did.] 'It was the coolest program I ever wrote.'
Bill Gates quoted in *Hard Drive* by James Wallace and Jim Erikson, 1992.

For the next eight weeks, Gates worked almost non-stop at the Harvard computer centre. He was adapting a computer language called BASIC – Beginners' All-purpose Symbolic Instruction Code. Allen, who had a job in Boston, joined him when he could. They were blazing a trail. No one had ever written code for a microcomputer before. Some people said it was not possible.

At the end of eight weeks Allen flew down to Albuquerque with the finished program. They had not even tested it because they could not get hold of an Altair 8800. Allen held his breath as he fed the program into MITS' computer. It worked first time.

Bill Gates with Paul Allen. Together, they co-founded Microsoft.

19

Micro-Soft

Not all new technology caught on. This touch screen computer looked good but people didn't find it as practical as keyboard functions. Later, the computer mouse did catch on.

Ed Roberts, the owner of MITS, was impressed. Not only did he agree to buy their program, he also offered Paul Allen a job as director of software. Allen moved to live in Albuquerque while Gates continued his studies at Harvard.

In April 1975 Gates and Allen formed the business partnership they had talked of at school. They called it Micro-Soft. Though Gates was still only nineteen, he showed his tough business sense in the deal with Roberts. He refused to sell the program outright. Instead he insisted on a licence, or leasing agreement. That gave MITS the exclusive right to sell the software with the Altair 8800. This has now become the standard, or usual, way of doing business in the world of computer software.

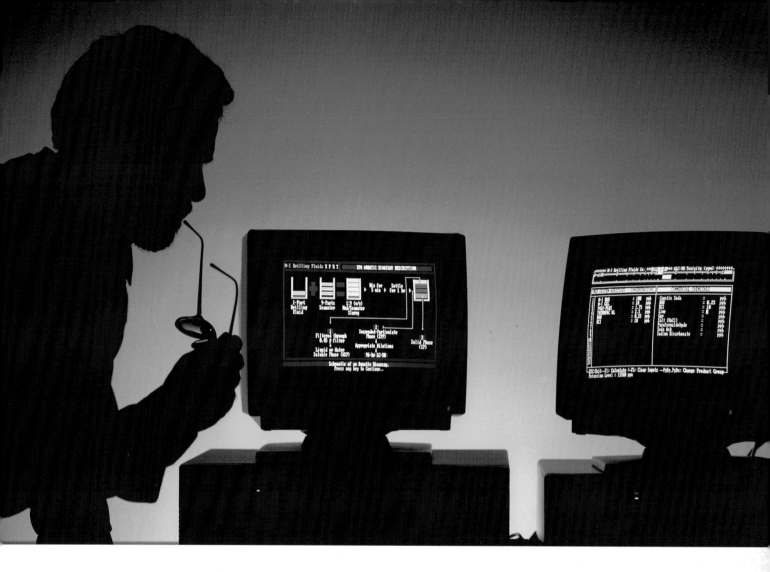

Demand was enormous. Paul Allen soon gave up his job with MITS to work full-time for Micro-Soft. Back at Harvard, Gates was torn apart. Should he finish his degree or strike out on his own? After much soul-searching, and against the wishes of his parents, he finally decided in favour of his new business. It was a decision he has not regretted.

By the 1980s the computer revolution was in full swing with the introduction of microcomputers. World-wide, offices were installing their first computers.

'Life for us was working, and maybe going to a movie, and then working some more. Sometimes we were so tired we would fall asleep in front of customers.'
Bill Gates, *New York Times*, 14 March 1995
talking about life at Albuquerque from 1976–79.

Fighting Spirit

The Micro-Soft team (Gates bottom left, Allen bottom right) pose for a photograph. Nearly all of them are just like Gates – young, male and mad about computers and software.

Neither Allen nor Gates had much time for Ed Roberts. Gates, in particular, thought Roberts ran his business badly. Roberts, for his part, thought Gates was a spoilt rich kid, who lost his temper when he did not get his own way. This is true. Even Gates admits that he shouts and calls people names when things go wrong. Added to this, Gates still looked about thirteen years old and had a high, squeaky voice. He was not taken seriously. There were frequent heated arguments.

The trouble was that Micro-Soft depended on MITS to sell their product. MITS soon stopped trying to sell the product because it was easy to make illegal copies of the software.

Gates realized that to make any real money, Micro-Soft had to break away from MITS. Then he could go after sales himself. There was a big legal battle lasting nine months and Micro-Soft nearly went out of business. In the end Micro-Soft won. Bill Gates breathed a sigh of relief. But it had taught him a valuable lesson about the need to be ruthless.

Gates continued to look younger than his age. But as soon as he started talking about computers, people were astounded at his knowledge.

'Most of you steal your software. Hardware must be paid for but software is something to share. Who cares if the people who worked on it get paid?' From Bill Gates' angry letter complaining about piracy published in a computer magazine in 1975.

The Big Break

The orders for software rolled in and Micro-Soft thrived. Sales soon topped $1 million a year. But it was difficult to get good programmers to move to Albuquerque. No one wanted to live in a backwater. So in 1979 Gates and Allen moved the company to Seattle. Their dozen employees moved with them. Micro-Soft lost the hyphen in its name, becoming Microsoft.

By this time the computer industry was 'going crazy'. It seemed everyone wanted to be part of the new industry. IBM was easily the biggest player in the computer market. So when the company approached Gates in 1980 about a program for their new personal computer, Gates sat up and took notice.

The Microsoft offices in Seattle are spread out over a large area. They are designed to make everyone feel on the same level, from the office cleaner to the company president.

By contrast, the IBM tower in Atlanta, Georgia, is a skyscraper. This older, more established company has many different levels.

To start with, IBM needed an operating system. Gates said he could have one ready within a year. He knew of a system he could buy and adapt. He paid just $75,000 for the system, modified it and called it MS-DOS, standing for Microsoft Disk Operating System. MS-DOS was sold with every IBM computer. But, learning from his previous experience with MITS, Gates retained the right to sell MS-DOS to other companies as well. Before long, Gates was selling MS-DOS to everyone.

The Appliance of Science

But the operating system was only half the story when it came to software. The IBM PC, and all the other computers, also needed an application.

An application turns a computer into a very specialized machine. If you install a word-processing application, you then have a word processor. Another application will turn the computer into a machine that deals with spreadsheets (for working out accounts). A third application might be a game. Gates realized the applications market was worth a great deal of money. He decided to get Microsoft heavily involved. With Bill Gates, there is always this drive to achieve more.

Microsoft employees relax outside the Microsoft offices at lunchtime.

Microsoft's Word program for word processors was launched in 1983. It was fast and very powerful. It had a mouse to point and click instead of using complex instructions on a keyboard. It also used colour pictures instead of words for some of the choices on the menu. It looked good and, even more important, it was very easy to use. Gates wanted everyone to own a computer. It was part of his vision of the future.

> **'Bill was furious when Lotus (a Microsoft competitor) came out with a spreadsheet programme that was better than ours. He knew that applications was where the money was.'**
> A programmer at Microsoft, 1983.

With the right applications, Bill Gates realized that computers could be used by the whole family, as well as by professionals and office workers.

Computer Wars

Microsoft was becoming a highly successful company. In 1985 it sold over $140 million worth of products and employed thousands of people. In 1986 the company was floated on the New York Stock Exchange. Gates became a dollar millionaire overnight. The following year he became the world's youngest ever billionaire.

The Microsoft executives (left to right) Jon Shirley, Bill Gates and Steve Ballmer in 1985.

Throughout the 1980s Microsoft devised software for IBM computers.

But Microsoft and Gates had made many enemies. Paul Allen, a more laid-back, relaxed man, retired from the business in 1982 because he became ill. This left Gates in sole charge. He was ruthless against competitors and he could be rude and sarcastic. Some companies refused to do business with Microsoft because their methods were so underhand. Apple even sued Microsoft in court for stealing some of their ideas. But Apple lost.

Perhaps the toughest battle was with IBM. Trust between the two companies broke down. In 1989 the partnership with IBM came to an end. Both sides blamed the other for the split. IBM decided to write its own software. Gates now found himself competing against the biggest computer company in the world, instead of selling to it.

Windows

Would Microsoft make it without IBM? As usual, Gates had an ace up his sleeve and he liked nothing better than a game of poker. Only this time, the stakes were millions of dollars.

The ace up Gates' sleeve was Windows. Gates gambled the whole future of Microsoft on this new system which replaced MS-DOS. Two earlier versions of Windows had already been released. Both failed to sell. But Windows 3.0, which came out in 1990, was a best seller. It was faster, more powerful and with much more space to store information. Now the computer could run several applications at the same time, so the user could switch from spreadsheets to a database or to writing a letter on a word processor with one point-and-click of the mouse. It allowed a 'window' into the different applications.

*Bill Gates receives a technical excellence award from **PC** Magazine in November, 1986.*

Still Gates pushed on. Windows 3.1 came out two years later with a thousand improvements. It was installed in 70 million personal computers in its first year. And 90 per cent of new computers were sold with the new program. IBM's product, OS/2, was completely outclassed by Windows.

'*Microsoft is now driving the industry, not IBM.*'
Fred Gibbons in *Wall Street Journal*, January 1991.

Gates took an enormous risk when he decided to continue to invest in Windows but this has become now one of the most familiar screen images in the world.

Marriage to Melinda

Just a week after their wedding the Gates' attended a party in their honour back home in Seattle. Gates is twisting the ring on his wedding finger, getting used to his new status as a married man.

Work always came first for Bill Gates. This left him little time for a social life or a girlfriend. But no one who knew him well ever doubted that he would one day get married.

Melinda French made a big impression on Gates when she joined Microsoft as a business manager in 1987. Nine years younger than Gates, she was born and grew up in Dallas, Texas and was able to cope with Gates' fiery personality!

This picture is of the secret marriage ceremony held on a cliff top overlooking the Pacific Ocean. Photographers were not supposed to take pictures but some obviously managed.

According to people who know Melinda she is 'funny, intelligent and very intense'. She is also obsessive about privacy. She will not talk to the press and has forbidden family and friends to talk publicly about her private life as well.

She and Gates dated on and off for several years before finally getting engaged in 1993. Gates showed a romantic streak by flying Melinda to Omaha, Nebraska, one Sunday morning. His friend Warren Buffett had Borsheim's, his jewellery store, opened specially for them so they could pick out a ring. They got married in Hawaii in January 1994.

'When I'm 35, I'll get married.' Bill Gates talking about marriage in *The Making of Microsoft* by Daniel Ichbiah and Susan L Knepper. He didn't marry Melinda until he was 38.

The World's Richest Man

Anyone expecting that marriage would slow Bill Gates down was in for a rude shock. His many competitors, and his enemies, were probably hoping that his python-like grip on the software market would ease off. Unhappily for them, the squeeze got tighter.

'This is my life. It's what I am. It's what I get excited about.'
Bill Gates talking about his work, *Sunday Times*, November 1999.

The launch of Windows 95 was delayed several times because it was vital to include an Internet browser. Here Gates is explaining how it works to customers in Seattle.

Windows had already virtually cornered the market when Windows 95 came out. But this latest operating system took computing much further. It was much faster than before. There was enough power to run booking systems for hotels and airlines. It could operate CD-ROMs, the fax machine, e-mail, the Internet. A technical problem had been corrected so the system did not crash so often. It would change the way people worked, shopped, gossiped, booked holidays and bought theatre tickets.

By the end of 1995 Gates was reckoned to be the world's wealthiest man. He owned $12.9 billion of Microsoft shares without even counting his annual income. He did all this without taking one cent from his parents.

Getting ready for lift-off! A Microsoft employee opens the Windows 95 program just before the release of the new software.

35

The Lakeside Home

It looks more like a building site than a home but the interior of the Lakeside house was completed when this photo was taken in September 1997.

So what kind of home would the world's richest man like to live in? To start with, it had to be big. It also had to be very private with lots of security. And, being a man with a vision of the future, Gates made sure everything was controlled by state-of-the-art computer technology.

The house has forty-five rooms in seven main pavilions linked by underground passageways. It stands on the shore of beautiful Lake Washington, surrounded by five acres of pleasant woodland. No one can get into the property without passing guards at the gate. It cost about $50 million and took seven years to build. Gates once said it felt as though he had been building a house all his life.

The property's 'brain' is a central computer room. This controls everything – the video-art walls, the doors that open and close and the lights that go on and off automatically. It also controls the music that follows you around the house, the temperature of the water in your bath, even the climate! Just in case the computer crashes, there are manual on-off switches as well.

'I wanted technology to play a role in a home that was handsome and practical and livable.'
Bill Gates, from *Bill Gates Speaks,* 1998.

BILL GATES
THE ROAD AHEAD

COMPANION INTERACTIVE CD-ROM INSIDE

This is the front cover of Gates' book, published in 1995. It will be interesting to see how many of his predictions for the future are correct.

Getting a Life

It was not long after their marriage in 1994 that children came along. Jennifer was born in 1996 and Rory in 1999. Fatherhood has genuinely changed Gates. Now if he is up all night, it is because he is caring for a crying baby, not looking for bugs on a computer program.

Gates' idea of relaxation is different from most other people's – he prefers to work long hours and doesn't need to switch off like most people do. This must be the secret of his greatness. Now Gates puts in only 12 hours a day at the office during the week and only 8 hours a day at weekends! Somehow he still finds time to read. His favourite works include the American novels *The Great Gatsby* and *Catcher in the Rye*.

Bill and Melinda Gates arrive at the Seattle Cinerama in April 1999. She is seven months pregnant with their second child.

Gates likes to wave his hands about while he is talking about something he thinks is important. Here he is at the White House Conference in April 2000.

He has always enjoyed fast cars. He usually drives a Porsche but also owns several Ferraris, a Lexus and a Jaguar XJ6. As a young man he collected many speeding tickets. One of his favourite ways of letting off steam was to drive fast at night in the desert round Albuquerque. These days he is more respectable. He likes to relax over a game of bridge with Warren Buffett, the world's second richest man, or a round of golf with former US president Bill Clinton.

> 'Time is the scarce resource and I treat it that way.'
> Bill Gates, *Bill Gates* by Lesinski.

Gates' best score at golf is 87. His ambition is to score 72 but he does not think he will achieve that.

Getting it Wrong

You don't become the richest person in the world by making lots of mistakes. This is certainly true of Bill Gates. He gets it wrong sometimes but he is very quick to spot errors. He also has the ability to learn from his mistakes.

Probably his biggest mistake was failing to see the importance of the Internet. Initially, Gates thought the Internet would not take off. Fortunately for him, he was persuaded to change his mind in 1994 by some of the younger employees at Microsoft. Within a year Microsoft launched Internet Browser as part of the Windows 95 package.

> **'The closest thing to it (the Internet) I can think of is the Gold Rush where everybody went off to find their fortune.'**
> Bill Gates in a speech at Learn Education Conference, Seattle, 30 June 1997.

Microsoft teamed up with Cisco Systems to produce new technology for using the Internet. Here Gates demonstrates an 'Internet telephone'.

Not everybody approves of Gates and his ways of doing business. This protest took place on the Microsoft campus in February 2000.

It was also possibly a mistake to make so many enemies, and to allow Microsoft to grow so big. The US government did not like one company becoming so powerful, with such a large share (about 95 per cent) of the computer software market. In 1998 Microsoft was taken to court by the Justice Department for illegal business practices. In June 2000 the judge ruled that Microsoft should be split up into two, smaller businesses. Gates has appealed against the decision.

In October 2000 Microsoft was in the news again when hackers managed to break in and copy secret codes for the software. Microsoft's reputation for security was badly damaged.

Distributing the Fortune

Gates' money is nearly all in Microsoft stock. Because the value of the stock changes from day to day, it is difficult to say exactly what he is worth. But on the 'unofficial' Bill Gates website is a 'wealth clock' showing how much money Bill Gates has at any given moment. On 13 February 2001 he was worth $67 billion.

In December 1998 the Gates announced they were giving US$100 million to establish a Children's Vaccine Programme for developing countries.

In 1999 Gates set up the Bill and Melinda Gates Foundation, currently worth $21 billion. It is the largest charitable trust in the world. Its aim is to support projects connected with world health and education. The Foundation has recently given $26 million to research a cure for malaria, a disease which kills millions of people in poor countries.

This is what makes it all worth while! Gates smiles with satisfaction as children at Rumah Faith Orphanage in Malaysia show him their homepages.

Another $200 million has gone to Cambridge University in England to help students study science and technology.

Gates aims to be the biggest single benefactor in history. He was deeply moved on a visit to Africa where he saw desperately poor children without enough food to eat. It made him realize that computers were not the answer to the problems of poverty and disease. It was a turning point in his life.

'*Mothers are going to walk right up to that computer and say to it, "My children are dying – what can you do about it?".*'
Gates speaking at a conference in Seattle in October 2000 on how computers are unable to help some people in the developing world.

The Shape of Things to Come

According to Gates, we are at the start of the Information Highway. It is difficult to imagine, but the Internet will soon be replaced by a far more powerful computer network called The Grid.

The Grid will be more secure and more reliable than the Internet. It will not be possible to infect it with viruses. Hackers will not be able to access secret information (as they did at Microsoft in October 2000). It will also be much, much bigger, rather like a 10-lane motorway compared with a country lane. Instead of going to the doctor, you will get a diagnosis and prescription via the screen and printer. People will pay for goods with a wallet-sized PC carried in a pocket. Everything will be digital.

Left: **Nelson Mandela, South Africa's first black President, made a big impression on Gates when they met at a Global Health Forum in Seattle in 1999. He admires the way Mandela thinks about politics and life.**

Right: **An electronic housedog is an example of what homes might contain in the future.**

Gates watches as one of his employees shows him a new video game console. The graphics are as realistic as a high-quality photograph.

As for Gates himself, he is still bubbling away with enthusiasm for the future. In June 2000 his company revealed their plans for Microsoft.NET. This will allow people to use the Internet with Microsoft software much more easily. But from time to time Gates has talked about retirement. So if anyone fancies a top job in computing, there may be one sometime soon at Microsoft!

'Picking that next person (to head up Microsoft) is something I give a lot of thought to. But it's probably five years before I have to do something very concrete about it.'
Bill Gates, *The Times*, 8 July 1998.

Glossary

Access To be allowed entry into something.

Autistic A mental condition where the person has difficulty communicating.

Charitable Not profit-making.

Complex Difficult to understand.

Cornered the market Taken all the sales.

Diagnosis A doctor's decision about the kind of illness or disease a person has.

Digital Operated by pressing buttons which represent certain information codes within the computer.

Gifted Extremely talented or intelligent.

Hacker Somebody who uses their skill with computers to gain illegal access to computer networks.

Hardware The mechanical and electronic parts of a computer.

Illegal Against the law.

Infect To spread disease.

Internet The international computer network, or World-Wide Web, which offers links between businesses, schools and individuals.

Internet browser A computer program which allows users access to the Internet.

Investigate Look into something.

Irregular Without a fixed pattern.

Laid-back Not aggressive, calm.

Leasing agreement A legal arrangement where a person pays to borrow a product for a given time.

Licence Permission to use a product for a particular purpose.

Marquees Large tents used for special occasions.

Mathematical formulae Sets of numbers used to define ideas in maths.

Memorized Learnt by heart.

Outclassed Beaten soundly by a competitor.

Pavilion A separate building.

Piracy Making an illegal copy of something, such as software.

Poker A game of cards.

Prescription A piece of paper from the doctor telling the chemist what medicines to give you.

Prosperous Wealthy, having plenty of money.

Respectable Having a good position in society.

Ruthless Without mercy, very determined.

Sarcastic Making fun of someone unkindly.

Self-made man Someone who made a lot of money after starting with nothing.

Software The programs and operating information used by a computer.

Specialized Adapted for a particular use.

Sued Made to go to court and threatened with having to pay out large sums of money.

University campus The grounds around a college or university.

Virus A computer program which is designed to destroy computer systems or computer data.

Date Chart

1955, October Bill Gates born, Seattle, Washington.

1967, September Gates starts at Lakeside School. Meets Paul Allen. Forms club called the Lakeside Programmers.

1971 Signs first business deal with C-Cubed.

1973 Graduates from Lakeside and starts at Harvard University.

1974 Allen sees Altair 8800 advertised in *Popular Electronics*.

1975 Allen and Gates sell first software program for a microcomputer. Allen is offered job with MITS. Gates and Allen form Micro-Soft. Gates leaves Harvard to concentrate on new business.

1977 Micro-Soft breaks away from MITS.

1979 Microsoft loses hyphen and moves to Seattle.

1980 IBM asks Microsoft to write software program for new PC.

1982 Allen resigns because of ill health.

1983 Microsoft launches Word program with colour pictures for choices and mouse to click and point.

1986 Microsoft is floated on New York Stock Exchange.

1987 Gates becomes world's youngest-ever billionaire aged thirty-two.

1989 Partnership with IBM breaks down.

1990 Windows 3.0 is launched.

1992 Windows 3.1 is launched.

1994 Marries Melinda French. Gates' mother dies from breast cancer.

1995 Launch of Windows 95. Becomes world's richest man, worth $12.9 billion. Publishes best-seller *The Road Ahead*.

1996 First child, Jennifer, is born.

1998 Sued by Justice Department.

1999 Second child, Rory, is born. Sets up Bill and Melinda Gates Foundation.

2000 Microsoft loses court action brought by Justice Department. Plans for Microsoft.NET are launched. Hackers break into Microsoft.

Further Information

Books for Younger Readers
Bill Gates by Sean Connolly
(Heinemann, 1999)

Books for Older Readers/Sources
Bill Gates by Robert Heller
(Dorling Kindersley, 2000)
Bill Gates and Microsoft by David Marshall
(Exley, 1994)

Bill Gates Speaks by Janet Lowe
(John Wiley and Sons, 1998)
Website addresses
http://www.microsoft.com/billgates/default.asp
Microsoft's official pages on Gates.
http://www.glf.org
Bill and Melinda Gates Foundation.

Index

Page numbers in **bold** mean there is a picture on the page.